PREACHING
to the
CHOIR

PREACHING
to the
CHOIR

Claiming the Role
of Sacred Musician

VICTORIA SIROTA

CHURCH PUBLISHING
an imprint of
Church Publishing Incorporated, New York

Scripture quotations unless otherwise noted are from the New
Revised Standard Version Bible, copyright © 1989 by the Division
of Christian Education of the National Council of the Churches
of Christ in the U.S.A., and are used by permission.

Library of Congress Cataloging-in-Publication Data

Sirota, Victoria Ressmeyer, 1949-
    Preaching to the choir : claiming the role of sacred musician /
Victoria Sirota.
      p. cm.
    ISBN-13: 978-0-89869-528-1
    ISBN-10: 0-89869-528-7
    1. Church music. 2. Church musicians. 3. Music – Religious
aspects – Christianity. 4. Music in churches. I. Title.
BV290.S57 2006
264'.2 – dc22
                              2006019668

Church Publishing Incorporated
445 Fifth Avenue
New York, NY 10016
www.churchpublishing.org

5 4 3 2 1

To Bob,
who talked me into transferring
from Oberlin College
to Oberlin Conservatory of Music

CONTENTS

PREFACE

Dear Reader,

This book arises from my journey as a church organist and choral conductor, as an officer and chaplain of the American Guild of Organists (AGO), as a member of the Association of Anglican Musicians (AAM), and as an Episcopal priest. The bulk of the material first appeared as articles in *The American Organist*, "From the Chaplain" (April 2000–July 2002).

I was raised in a Missouri Synod Lutheran parsonage, and so the surprise of my life has been the call to ordained ministry in the Episcopal Church. While that is not the topic of the present volume, I must say that my spiritual journey from the organ bench and podium to the pulpit has profoundly influenced my view of the role of the sacred musician in religious institutions, and for these insights I am grateful to God.

This book is designed to aid the musician working in a church or synagogue, as well as to inform those with whom they work and serve about the unique issues they face. While my direct experience includes playing services in Lutheran, Methodist, Congregational, Episcopal, Unitarian, and interdenominational venues, my prayer is that the issues raised will be helpful to musicians in any religious context.

I am grateful to many of you who have encouraged and inspired me over the years: the faithful and loving choirs, congregation, clergy, and staff at Epiphany Episcopal Church in Winchester, Massachusetts, and especially at St. Paul's Episcopal Church in Dedham, Massachusetts; the wonderful students and colleagues I have been blessed to have at Concord Academy, Boston University, Yale Divinity School and Institute of Sacred Music, and at the Ecumenical Institute of Theology at St. Mary's Seminary and University; and friends and colleagues in denominational gatherings and at AGO and AAM local, regional, and national meetings and conventions.

A special thanks goes to the late Dr. Philip Hahn, who appointed me national chaplain for the American Guild of Organists during his tenure as national president (1998–2002). The overwhelming response to my columns as chaplain has forced me to take this all the more seriously, and I am grateful to Anthony Baglivi and his staff at *The American Organist* for their support and guidance.

I also wish to thank my organ teachers and professors: Oscar Magnusson (Grace Lutheran Church, Malverne, New York), Garth Peacock (Oberlin Conservatory of Music), André Marchal (Paris), Gustav Leonhardt (Amsterdam), and George Faxon (Boston

University), each of whom revealed a different side of the divine mystery of playing the organ. I am grateful to Harvard Divinity School and to Professors Margaret R. Miles, John Carmen, Richard R. Niebuhr, and especially Richard Valantasis and Peter Gomes for helping me find my voice. "Claim your authority," Valantasis would say. Sister Carolyn Darr, mother superior of St. Margaret's Convent in Boston and former president of AAM, has blessed me with her discernment and intense prayer life. And I am grateful to Church of the Holy Nativity, an Episcopal urban mission church in northwest Baltimore, for teaching me what is truly important this side of eternity.

Religious communities whose liturgical lives have had a profound effect on my thinking in addition to the places where I have been employed as musician or priest include: Church of St. John the Evangelist, Boston, during the co-rectorship of the Reverends Jennifer Phillips and Richard Valantasis; St. Mary's Episcopal Church, Dorchester, Massachusetts, under the Reverend Edward O. Waldron; and St. Margaret's Convent in Boston under the liturgical leadership of Sister Carolyn Darr.

I am grateful to my editor, Marilyn Haskel, for her interest in this book from the beginning. She has been a true collaborator. The manuscript has benefited greatly from her added insight as a sacred musician. Thanks also to Karen Amrhein, who donated her copying services for an early version of the hymn "O Holy Nativity."

I wish to thank my parents, the Reverend Henry Ressmeyer and Ruth Bretscher Ressmeyer, who have passed on a profound love of Christ, knowledge, beauty, and music; my siblings Christa Ressmeyer Klein, Georgia Ressmeyer, and Roger Ressmeyer, who have helped me process this legacy with their own added intensity and humor; my Jewish in-laws, the Sirota family, who have enlarged my worldview, love me as their own, and keep me laughing; my son, Jonah, his wife, Kate Maattala, and my daughter, Nadia, who amaze me with their talent, intellect, wisdom, and passion; and my husband Robert Sirota, who has helped me in untold ways and who has had the courage to stand with me at the abyss and seek the Holy One.

Finally, I wish you to know that I am praying for you. If this book touches you, I pray that you pass on musically whatever words of healing, comfort, or inspiration you find here. This weary world needs your gifts. We are all listening.

Victoria Ressmeyer Sirota
Holy Week 2006

INTRODUCTION

YOU HURL YOURSELF upstairs to the organ loft, late to start the prelude because of the choir's tardiness at the final rehearsal of the elaborate offertory anthem. As you settle yourself on the bench, you realize you forgot to find a page turner. Too late now. There go the continuous sixteenth notes in the left hand at the bottom of the third and fifth pages. You consider playing the prelude faster than you have practiced it in order to get it all in — or should you cut it? Where would a cut make logical sense and not destroy the architecture? Or should you just let it run its proper length and risk the ire of the minister, who has a cow when the service begins late? You pull stops or press pistons. Your hands and feet find their rightful positions.

But here is the moment — the moment when the creative voice will begin to sing out over the random cough, the restless silence. Do you remember to take a deep breath? Do you remember to pray the music into existence?

Being the musician of a religious institution can be a lonely experience. Many parishioners take you for granted or grumble behind your back. The comments may range from "Why do you play Bach all the time?" or "Why do you just play that French music?" to "Why isn't the choir bigger?" "The hymns are too fast," "Do you let just anyone into the choir?" or "You make the organ sound so terrific, why do we need to renovate it?"

Many factors figure into your choice of repertoire: the strengths and weaknesses of the volunteer or professional choir, or of the particular instrument at hand; the amount of time you will have to rehearse or practice that week; key relationships and mood; and the character of the liturgy that day. The quality of the worship experience will be influenced by you as musician (whether organist, choir director, cantor, soloist, or instrumentalist) as well as by the many other people in leadership roles (including lay readers, ushers, eucharistic ministers, deacons, rabbis, preachers, and ministers) and how you interact with each other. For all of you, your physical, emotional, and spiritual states, as well as your ability to be truly present, hold significance.

While the expression "Preaching to the Choir" implies an unnecessary exhortation to the sacred musician, the importance of good music for transcendent worship suggests that the intentionality of preaching to the choir is exactly what is needed. Many of the music leaders with whom I have conversed over the years complain that they are not receiving the encouragement and inspiration they need in their church or synagogue to continue to do their best work.

The sacred musician holds the profound responsibility of helping the congregation find its voice. This is no minor role. The myriad tasks of organist, cantor, and choir director are diverse and complex. It is easy to lose sight of what is most important. The passion, dexterity, and leadership of this musician have everything to do with joyful and healthy worship. In addition, if the post represents the most significant salaried lay position, there are further responsibilities to nurture the discourse between the ordained leadership and the laity.

> *Being the musician of a religious institution can be a lonely experience.*

Great musicians (performers and conductors) work hard on seamless continuity — on choreographing all of their movements so that they add to the musical intention and do not distract. Religious musicians add their own spirituality to the mix. Through the transparent choices of tempo, organ registration, dynamics, genre, and style of music, the congregation discovers who the musician is and what the musician believes. In the best liturgical experiences, the spirituality of the musician complements the spirituality of the worshiping community and helps to carry the gathered faithful into the awesome presence of the Almighty. The hymns are sung with zest and passion. The silences are profound. As a result, the clergy and lay leaders are inspired to share a deeper part of themselves in the way they read scriptures, preach, or pray. The Spirit is clearly present.

Allowing the Spirit to be present and not getting in the way is the goal. This involves an integration of gift, talent, skill, and intention. The musician who is able to claim the call that motivates the work connects profoundly with an interior compass, an ethical core. In this inner shrine, there is gratitude for the presence of the Divine and for the gifts that have been bestowed. In this place of peace, there will also be compassion for others. The purpose of this book is to hold up the profession of the sacred musician in a way that sheds new light on the issues, elicits a greater understanding of the forces that work with and against the musician, and encourages a deeper commitment to claim the call that first brought us to this holy place.

So back to the organ bench. This time you say a quick prayer: You ask for help. You are in over your head. You feel inadequate to the task. And yet you wish this offering to be truly inspired. You pray that the Spirit will infuse these notes with the breath of God. You lift your hands. The music begins. . . .

One

CLAIMING THE CALL
OF SACRED MUSICIAN

HOW DO YOU claim the call of sacred musician? Some people know from early on that this is their true identity; others fall into a church or temple position quite surprisingly. No matter how you find yourself to be employed as a sacred musician, there comes a time when it may be helpful, or even vital, for you to discover whether this actually is a "calling." The first inkling may be the moment you realize you no longer are doing it just for the money. You find yourself playing the organ, conducting the choir, or singing the Lord's praises because you have felt God's delight in you as you share these musical gifts with others. You have discovered that making music on sacred ground makes you happier than anything else on earth in the deepest place of your soul.

The decision to take music lessons (the first step) is separate from the decision to devote your life to becoming a musician and artist (the second step). After years of lessons comes the determination as to whether this is how you want to spend your life, or whether this will always be a sideline or hobby for you. Gifts, talents, self-discipline, and level of commitment need to be assessed and weighed against abilities and interests in other areas. The opinions of other excellent musicians matter as well. How do they see you? The question to ask yourself is not just, "Can I pass the audition in order to get into a higher level of training?" but "Can I live without making music?"

The third step is similar but slightly different — discerning whether you are *called* to perform on the concert stage or in the sanctuary. Musicians are trained to play for applause. This is considered a good thing. Sacred musicians, however, answer to a higher power. The goal is not just to please the people but also to please God. The call of sacred musician involves empowering the congregation to feel the divine presence, helping them to raise their voices in praise, and inspiring them with a taste of heaven. This is a tall order.

The level of self-discipline is huge. There is never enough practice time. Repertoire needs to be learned quickly and used weekly. In addition to a working knowledge of organ and choral repertoire, service music, and different liturgical settings and styles, the musician needs to understand and oversee the repair and tuning of organs and pianos, connect with the needs of the congregation, rehearse and inspire the choirs — all working at different performing levels — and attend meetings with clergy and staff. Larger positions also involve hiring and rehearsing instrumentalists and other musicians for special occasions, and often composing and arranging parts for them. Frequently the salary and benefits are not commensurate with the expectations for the position. Why would anyone choose this willingly?

Because you feel called. Because when you accompany the hymn and everyone is singing God's praises together, you are filled with emotion. Because you are struck time and again by how miraculous it is that this ordinary volunteer choir can sound so extraordinary. Because you love the profound silence that fills the room when the last notes of a great composition are sent heavenward. Because nothing makes you feel more alive. Because you know you are standing in the presence of the Almighty.

So if you are called by God to be a musician in the House of the Lord, then why is the job so difficult? Why is there often tension with the clergy and problems with the choir and congregation?

Remember that to work for God requires a genuine relationship with the Divine. It is not possible for a mere mortal to have this relationship without conflict and tension. Read the Psalms: "O Lord, do not rebuke me in your anger, or discipline me in your wrath. For your arrows have sunk into me, and your hand has come down on me" (Ps. 38:1–2). "My God, my God, why have you forsaken me? Why are you so far from helping me, from the words of my groaning?" (Ps. 22:1). Read the prophets. Read the laments of Jeremiah. The disciples and early apostles struggled mightily even as they proclaimed the good news.

Remember also that where God is, evil is never very far. Spiritual warfare is part of any authentic spiritual journey. The temptations to be wooed by position or power, to claim all of the credit for yourself, to forget to pray, to neglect to ask for help, to prefer to feel alone and filled with self-pity are easy traps. Even Jesus was tempted by the devil in the wilderness to misuse his gifts, test his relationship with God, and seek power and glory.[1]

Screwtape, a veteran devil created by the English writer C. S. Lewis, encourages the young devils in training in "Screwtape Proposes a Toast" with his final words: "All said and done, my friends, it will be an ill day for us if what most humans mean by 'religion' ever vanishes from the Earth. It can still send us the truly delicious sins. The fine flower of unholiness can grow only in the close neighborhood of the Holy. Nowhere do we tempt so successfully as on the very steps of the altar."[2] Anyone who works in sacred space can expect the assault. Do not be surprised. And do not be so naive as to think that you are somehow above the battle. What musicians, clergy, wardens, elders, and laity have in common are struggles with ego and idolatry — the need to be in control, have power, and be adored. The only way that real community can ever happen is to learn to pray with each other and give that power back to God.

How can you personally deal with evil? Know yourself. Get counseling, therapy, or spiritual direction as necessary. You need to be able to process your difficulties and struggles, your life scars and anger with a neutral party who can help you see where you are at fault and where you are not. Once you begin to understand better the forces with which you are contending, you will know how to pray. You will also better understand whether sacred musician remains the role to which God is calling you.

> *Remember also that where*
> *God is, evil is never very far.*

Calls are always time sensitive. Our desire to remain in the same place long after we have accomplished what we were sent to do may stem from habit, laziness, or lack of faith. Our Creator knows our specific gifts and talents, and has use for them. Sometimes the difficulties we encounter are an indication that it is simply time to move on.

An indication of good emotional and spiritual health is feeling genuine compassion for others, especially those whom you may have considered to be your enemies. If you are able to acknowledge your own weaknesses, you will become more tolerant of others.

You are human. God does not require perfection from you, but rejoices when you are faithful — when you have the courage to ask for forgiveness and return to the fold.

Working for the Almighty means that part of your calling is to do battle with evil — not necessarily evil people but evil ideas and thoughts, those that despise beauty and creativity — and stand up for what is good, right, and true. Therefore, do not forget to protect yourself. As the Apostle Paul writes to the Ephesians:

> Finally, be strong in the Lord and in the strength of his power. Put on the whole armor of God, so that you may be able to stand against the wiles of the devil. For our struggle is not against enemies of blood and flesh, but against the rulers, against the authorities, against the cosmic powers of this present darkness, against the spiritual forces of evil in the heavenly places. Therefore take up the whole armor of God, so that you may be able to withstand on that evil day, and having done everything, to stand firm. (Eph. 6:10–13)

Claiming your call as a sacred musician will provide you with the authority you need to do your work courageously. Figuring out what support systems you need to establish in order to do your best work will help you to do your work joyfully.

Two

MUSIC AS THEOLOGY

I N THE MOVIE *Master and Commander*, based on the novel by Patrick O'Brian, there is a wonderful moment when the HMS *Surprise* reaches the Galapagos Islands. We have been prepared for this by conversation about the possibility of new species of animals and insects never seen before by Europeans or by the scientific community. When the islands are reached, the camera provides a panoramic view as a single cello plays a movement from one of the Bach unaccompanied cello suites.[1] The result is breathtaking. The music provides the sense of awe and wonder that this new vista inspires. It helps us feel, and immediately brings us to a place of profound amazement. Johann Sebastian Bach (1685–1750), of course, did not write that music with this movie in mind. There is no text underlying the suite other than the name of the dance movement. Despite the fact that this piece is deemed a secular work, we hear something deeper. Somehow Bach encoded his faith, curiosity, and hope within it. What we hear (or think we hear) is his delight in the sheer gift of God's handiwork, his awe and wonder at being alive, his

23

gratitude to his Creator. Thus, the film benefits greatly from Bach's spirituality.

Different kinds of music perform different functions. Texted music is used, for example, to sell products on radio or television (advertising jingles), or arouse patriotism (national anthems). Untexted music (absolute music) is employed by many composers as the vehicle for some of their most profound and significant musical thought, such as symphonies and string quartets.

How did Bach pass along this message of awe and wonder without using words? This is one of the great mysteries of music. What this simple example reveals is that music exists as a "text" (in this case a non-verbal text) separate from words. The music itself conveys meaning. Therefore, it can be used to either reinforce or contradict any words that accompany it. Looking at it in this way, music becomes more than just a vehicle for theology; music *is* theology.

Because the composer's intention is not always clear in absolute music, I have chosen to use examples of music set to words to discuss the differences between the two. The questions then become: "Do the words and music say the same thing?" "Does the composer succeed in saying musically what the words imply?" or, "What aspect of the text is the composer addressing?" This kind of discussion begins to disclose the various layers of encoded meaning, both verbal and non-verbal, that we experience as audience, congregation, musician, theologian, and artist.

At a conference on music as theology in 1992,[2] Max Stackhouse played a recording of Leonard Bernstein's "There's a place for us"[3] from *West Side Story*. In the context of the Broadway show, this song at first represents the hope of new love for an earthly paradise that, tragically, comes to be revealed as unattainable. The Stephen Sondheim text allows for another meaning, however, and after Tony's death the reprise of the song gains further poignancy by expressing what has now become, as Stackhouse pointed out, an "eschatological hope." Besides the transfiguring beauty of the music and the performance, there were at least two other layers of meaning for me at this particular hearing that increased my emotional response.

The first was the memory of Bernstein, who loved to work with students, conducting the Tanglewood Music Center Orchestra barely two months before he died. As he walked on and off stage, it was evident that he was having difficulty breathing, but when he conducted the orchestra, the performance was as vigorous as ever and deeply profound. I found myself thinking that the eschatological hope expressed in "There's a place for us" was Bernstein's hope as a young man, and I reflected on his tortuous spiritual journey as it had been revealed to us in his life and music.

At the same time, I was experiencing parental separation anxiety as I remembered that my fifteen-year-old son was playing the suite from *West Side Story* in a youth orchestra touring Berlin, Prague, and Salzburg even as the conference was meeting. This was his first trip abroad. At the pre-tour concert at Symphony Hall in Boston, my husband and I had both cried when we heard this melody played with deep passion and conviction by talented adolescents of mixed races who have not yet become disillusioned with the imperfections inherent in earthly existence.

I cite these two extra-musical associations that are emotionally charged not because they are unusual, but because a great work of art will always evoke such associations. An emotionally powerful artistic creation that deals openly with cosmic issues of love and death will attract other extra-musical associations to it. If we had gone around the room at that conference sharing the most powerful recollection that "Somewhere" represented to us, I think that we would have been surprised at the intensity of response that exists just below the surface and is not often verbalized.

The musicologist Paul Henry Lang stated at the Fifth International Church Music Congress in 1966, "Art, like religion, elevates man, and even if he does not understand the immense culture that is encompassed in a masterpiece, he feels it."[4] It is in the ability to transmit a feeling, an emotion, that music and the arts are

26

unparalleled. Music enables us to experience as a corporate entity the same emotion at the same time. Through this, our deepest yearning for community is realized. We literally become "one body."

Although I did not share my intense emotional response to "There's a place for us" with anyone at the time, I did not feel embarrassed by my tears because I suspected that everyone was experiencing a similar stirring of their deepest emotions. Reading the text by itself may or may not have done that for us. Indeed, the text could sound rather shallow and silly if it were read by someone who was not interested in embracing his or her deepest emotions at that moment. Bernstein's music is a "reading" of the text that is clear in its attempt to engage the passions and to struggle with cosmic issues. The musician can count on the fact that if he or she plays the music as Bernstein has composed it, the performance will have an emotional impact.

Perhaps looking at two different pieces of music commonly set to the same words will highlight even more clearly the signification of the music apart from the verbal text. For this discussion, I have chosen to do a musical analysis of two settings of the Christmas carol "O Little Town of Bethlehem," which has the advantages of being short, self-contained, and well known.

The text by Phillips Brooks is paired with two different melodies in The Hymnal 1982 (see the illustrations of hymns 78 and 79 that follow),[5] both of which have

27

Hymn 78

Unison or harmony

1 O lit - tle town of Beth - le - hem, how still we see thee lie!
2 For Christ is born of Ma - ry; and gath - ered all a - bove,
3 How si - lent - ly, how si - lent - ly, the won - drous gift is given!
*4 Where child - ren pure and hap - py pray to the bless - ed Child,
5 O ho - ly Child of Beth - le - hem, de - scend to us, we pray;

1 A - bove thy deep and dream - less sleep the si - lent stars go by;
2 while mor - tals sleep, the an - gels keep their watch of won - dering love.
3 So God im - parts to hu - man hearts the bless - ings of his heaven.
4 where mis - er - y cries out to thee, Son of the mo - ther mild;
5 cast out our sin and en - ter in, be born in us to - day.

1 yet in thy dark streets shin - eth the ev - er - last - ing Light;
2 O morn - ing stars, to - geth - er pro - claim the ho - ly birth!
3 No ear may hear his com - ing, but in this world of sin,
4 where char - i - ty stands watch - ing and faith holds wide the door,
5 We hear the Christ - mas an - gels the great glad tid - ings tell;

1 the hopes and fears of all the years are met in thee to - night.
2 and prais - es sing to God the King, and peace to men on earth.
3 where meek souls will re - ceive him, still the dear Christ en - ters in.
4 the dark night wakes, the glo - ry breaks, and Christ - mas comes once more.
5 O come to us, a - bide with us, our Lord Em - man - u - el!

Words: Phillips Brooks (1835–1893)
Music: *Forest Green*, English melody; adapt. and harm. Ralph Vaughan Williams (1872–1958),
Copyright Oxford University Press. Used by Permission.

Hymn 79

1 O lit-tle town of Beth-le-hem, how still we see thee lie!
2 For Christ is born of Ma - ry; and gath-ered all a - bove,
3 How si - lent - ly, how si - lent - ly, the won-drous gift is given!
*4 Where child - ren pure and hap - py pray to the bless-ed Child,
5 O ho - ly Child of Beth-le-hem, de - scend to us, we pray;

1 A - bove thy deep and dream-less sleep the si - lent stars go by;
2 while mor-tals sleep, the an - gels keep their watch of won-dering love.
3 So God im-parts to hu - man hearts the bless-ings of his heaven.
4 where mis - er - y cries out to thee, Son of the mo - ther mild;
5 cast out our sin and en - ter in, be born in us to - day.

1 yet in thy dark streets shin-eth the ev - er - last - ing Light;
2 O morn - ing stars, to - geth - er pro - claim the ho - ly birth!
3 No ear may hear his com - ing, but in this world of sin,
4 where char - i - ty stands watch-ing and faith holds wide the door,
5 We hear the Christ - mas an - gels the great glad tid - ings tell;

1 the hopes and fears of all the years are met in thee to - night.
2 and prais - es sing to God the King, and peace to men on earth.
3 where meek souls will re - ceive him, still the dear Christ en - ters in.
4 the dark night wakes, the glo - ry breaks, and Christ - mas comes once more.
5 O come to us, a - bide with us, our Lord Em - man - u - el!

Words: Phillips Brooks (1835–1893)
Music: *St. Louis*, Lewis H. Redner (1831–1908)

their ardent supporters. Written for a Sunday School Christmas festival in 1868,[6] the hymn can be sung to the English melody "Forest Green" as adapted and harmonized by Ralph Vaughan Williams, or to "St. Louis" composed for Brooks by his organist Lewis H. Redner. The melodies have different flavors, each emphasizing a different side of the text.

"Forest Green" is in F major, diatonic in nature (no accidentals), and contrasts quarter notes with quicker eighth notes in each phrase, with the third phrase reversing this rhythmic motive. Phrases one, two, and four are virtually identical, beginning on a low dominant pitch (5 or C) and resolving to the tonic (1 or F) by means of an authentic cadence (V-I). Phrase three reverses this process as well, beginning on the tonic pitch and ending on the dominant in a half cadence (ii[6]-vi-V), thereby requiring the resolution of the last phrase, which provides a strong sense of closure (A-A-B-A). A number of secondary triads (ii, vi, iii) are used throughout for contrasting color, but they are strongly resolved by primary triads (I-IV-V).

There are relatively few skips between adjacent pitches in the first, second, and fourth phrases (only three out of sixteen). Phrase three employs twice as many (six out of eighteen), although the skips are still limited to those within the tonic triad (pitches 1, 3, and 5). This means that the melody moves largely by step and is relatively easy to sing. The upbeat beginning of the first phrase followed by a thrice-repeated tonic pitch provides the melody with an exuberant folk-song quality that is reinforced by eighth notes dancing the tune up to its high note.

From a theological standpoint, this music well depicts the joy of the angels and the morning stars proclaiming the "holy birth" in verse 2, but it does not really succeed in setting the profound silence of verses 1 and 3. The "world of sin" (v. 3) in this musical rendition does not seem at all frightening. There is no conflict between earth and heaven. We are singing with the angels as if we are all happy children. The darkness is already over. Christ is here.

"St. Louis" is quite different. Typical of nineteenth-century musical composition, it employs chromaticism in both the melody (measures 1 and 13) and harmony (measures 1, 2, 5, 7, 9, 10, 12, 13, 14, 15), more non-chord tones than "Forest Green," and a slower harmonic rhythm. (Measure 1 is a repeated tonic triad with two accented lower neighbor notes on beat three. Measure 2 is a ii chord in first inversion rather unusually preceded by three non-chord tones on the downbeat [two appoggiaturas and an accented chromatic passing tone]). The melody is bolder and more difficult to sing, employing intervallic skips of both major and minor thirds (4), perfect fourths (3), perfect fifths (2), major and minor sixths (4), as well as an octave.

In this hymn, phrase three is contrasting in that it moves to the relative minor key (d minor) and employs only repeated notes and movement by step instead of repeated notes and motion by step *and skip* as in the other phrases. Soprano and bass move in contrary motion in the first half of this phrase. In the second half, the lack of harmony for three notes (soprano, alto, tenor, and bass sing octaves) emphasizes the minor mode. The half cadence in d (iv⁶-V) slides back to the F major sonority at the beginning of the fourth phrase by common-tone modulation (the pitch A holds while the alto E moves to F, the tenor C-sharp moves to C-natural, and the bass A moves to F).

> *If the Spirit of God resides in the breath, then music . . . is a manifestation of that spirit.*

There is an introspective aspect to this melody and harmonization that is dreamier and more mystical, and seems to hold a stronger sense of awe for the Divine. One can believe the story surrounding the composition of "St. Louis" that tells of Redner's frustration with his inability to compose anything worthy of the words. Only at the last minute was he said to have been inspired with this music in a dream.[7] Because of the interesting melodic intervals and change of harmonies, the music requires a different kind of listening in order to sing it well. We become aware of the deep silence of the night and how we long for God. The slithering chromaticism and many leaps of the first two phrases seem to represent worldly distractions. The "everlasting Light" (v. 1), "morning stars" (v. 2), and "Christmas angels" (v. 5) of the third phrase return us to the basic unadorned line. Now we are ready to take the biggest leap of all (an octave), and request the presence of "our Lord, Emmanuel" (v. 5).

The music closely parallels the text and is more successful than "Forest Green" at setting the conflicting human feelings of fear, awe, and yearning that would be present for those actually witnessing the entrance of Christ on earth. The desire for a relationship with Jesus as intimate as that of Mary's birthing the "holy Child of Bethlehem" is sincerely expressed in v. 5. The music of "St. Louis" knows the darkness well, and yet is able to reach out to the light.

I remember having an impassioned argument a number of years ago with the priest at the church for which I was the musician. The issue was which of these two tunes we should use for the Christmas services. I felt strongly that "St. Louis" should be used, although at the time I had no theological basis to support my opinion. "St. Louis" was simply the nostalgic tune from my childhood. The priest argued for "Forest Green" for a similar reason. Our compromise was to use one tune on Christmas Eve and the other on Christmas Day.

As I look back at this kind of clergy/organist exchange, I find myself slightly embarrassed that I was not more sensitive to the many layers of meaning that our conversation was uncovering. We were both expressing insecurity, recollecting past Christmas experiences (both good and bad), and feeling the need to be "ministered to" as we faced the strain of being caregivers to others at a difficult time of year. For me, "Forest Green" was a lovely tune that had no Christmas connotation. For the priest, "St. Louis" appeared to have strong negative connotations (for whatever undisclosed reason). After having analyzed the music in relationship to the text, I am beginning to understand that the concrete confrontation with darkness in "St. Louis" (which does not happen in "Forest Green") may also have been informing our disparate responses.

It is important to add here that the performance makes a difference. The choice of tempo and registration, for example, add another layer of interpretation. It is possible to play "Forest Green" so slowly and softly that the minor secondary triads are emphasized in a way that does better justice to the mystery and awe represented in the text. Conversely, one can perform "St. Louis" so quickly and loudly that the listener misses its chromatic connection with the text's darkness and silence. Careful analysis of the significations of music and words and how they inform each other can help to lead the musician to a more profound rendition.

The issue of music as theology cannot be neglected. In her book *The Breath of God: An Approach to Prayer,* Nancy Roth speaks of the Spirit of God as residing in the breath. She reminds us that the word "spiritual" comes from the Latin word *spiritus,* which means both "breath" and "spirit," as does the Hebrew word *ruach* and the Greek word *pneuma.*[8] If the Spirit of God resides in the breath, then music, which allows us to breathe together as one body, is a manifestation of that spirit. Textual theology (reading the scripture, for example) is only one modality in which religious truths are revealed to us. In the liturgy, revelation comes through many different modes: through tasting, smelling, seeing, touching, feeling, and hearing. The whole body wants to respond to God's invitation for intimacy.

Openness to music, to listening for the Spirit, puts us in a more open posture for receiving divine revelation. The discourse between ministers and musicians reflects the inherent tension between the word and music, the spoken and unspoken, or the Word (as in John 1:1) and the Spirit. The congregation requires the use of both hemispheres of the brain, engaging the entire dialectic, in order to worship. By balancing and using all of the gifts that have been given to us, we are brought closer to each other and closer to the divine mystery.

In the Hellenistic and Greco-Roman ascetic literature of the first to the eleventh centuries C.E., the singing of hymns and psalms is a constant feature of ascetic discipline. The goals of this practice include healing and protection (self-revelation), self-forgetfulness, and becoming one with God. In this third category, singing the psalms gives way to a deep interior singing, which is actually silence. A powerful seventh-century Syriac text on prayer attributed to Abraham of Nathpar discusses how exterior singing can lead to the interior singing of "spiritual beings":

> For until someone has worshipped for a considerable time in this exterior manner — employing continual fasting, using the voice for psalmody, with repeated periods on his knees, . . . along with a careful watch over the senses, being filled with the remembrance of God, full of due fear and trembling at his name, seeing that he has a firm belief that the rustling movements of his thoughts are not hidden from God's knowledge, humbling himself before everyone, . . . when someone can do all this, and achieve it in himself, he will arrive at singing to God in the psalmody that spiritual beings use to praise him. For God is silence, and in silence is he

36

sung and glorified by means of that psalmody and praise of which he is worthy.[9]

By calming the body, mind, and soul the ascetic is no longer affected by angels or demons. The only movement is the reflection of the Divine. Through a deep, interior singing, the ascetic achieves union with God.

Music may be a vehicle for theology in "exterior singing," but it *is* theology in "interior singing." Like the ascetic, the artist/composer/musician struggles to overcome the needs of self in order to uncover a greater truth. Great works of art engage cosmic issues and eschatological hopes and are, therefore, in touch with that deep interior singing that is the divine voice. They allow us to know God directly through our senses. The community resonates with the Spirit of God. When we are the closest to each other, we are also the closest to being at one with God.

Music as a non-verbal expression should not be devalued because it cannot be adequately verbalized. As Edward Farley states, music can pull us out of ourselves and into community, moving us into the world of the Other, of "Thou."[10] Limiting our conversation to one side of the dialectic not only is unscholarly, but it also limits revelation. Being open to "other," other people as well as other modes of communication, is being open to the fullness of the creation and, therefore, to the fullness of God.

Three

THE SPIRITUALITY
OF THE SACRED MUSICIAN

L ET'S TALK ABOUT those amazing moments when an extraordinary musical experience happens in liturgical space. Every once in a while the performance of an inspired composition, whether old or new, connects text with musicians, choir, clergy, building, and congregation in a phenomenal way, as if all that is good and true in the universe is in cosmic alignment. For whatever reason, each person involved is united in the mission of this particular musical offering. Somehow egos have been put aside, the composer's whisperings are in the air, and the Spirit has brought the music to a more profound place than was ever thought possible. At the end of the experience, everyone knows that they have been transported to a different place and time. Those listening may be in tears; those performing shaken to the core of their being. What exactly has happened? Maybe the best way to describe that experience is that we have been where heaven and earth meet, a liminal place.[1] This is a "thin place" at the edge of the reality the world would claim as the only truth, where we suddenly glimpse Reality or, perhaps, Infinitude. It is here that we are able, however briefly, to see into the very heart of God. We know this place sometimes in intense prayer or meditation. That brief moment upon opening our eyes, when we have no idea where we are, is an indication that we have been there. Or perhaps we have experienced it while sitting in the presence of a deeply spiritual person who is dying, where every utterance is fraught with meaning, and the very air seems dense with angelic hosts and the communion of saints. We human beings may resist entering that unitive state of body, mind, and soul, but once experienced, we never want to leave.

I believe that our best musicians are mystics. The mystic seeks union with God beyond the intellectual and human experience. Evelyn Underhill writes in her classic work *Mysticism*, "All artists are of necessity in some measure contemplative. In so far as they surrender themselves without selfish preoccupation, they see Creation from the point of view of God."[2] The contemplative world of the musician, the world of practice and self-discipline, will give rise to the mystical experience, providing the musician can move beyond ego and narcissism.

Our society looks to music and the arts for mystical inspiration. The greatest artists and composers are always ahead of their time because the revelation that they are receiving, while inspired by the music and performances of the past, is as unique and singular as the individual soul who carries it forth. The process of giving birth to any creative idea may be a stormy one because the artist walks between two worlds, carrying messages from one side to another. This is not an easy task. And the average listener cannot be expected to absorb fully this revelation on first hearing, but needs to spend time in this new sound world in order to get used to it, to hear the beauty of new sonorities that may sound downright ugly to an uninitiated ear. With time and space, the music will find its place in the universe, and we, the listeners, will begin to appreciate the novelty of expression and the profundity of the encoded message. Underhill writes, "Often when we blame our artists for painting ugly things, they are but striving to show us a beauty to which we are blind."[3]

The gift of being an artist is the ability to express the inexpressible. Mystical visions do not lend themselves to scientific treatises. Underhill states, "Here poet, mystic, and musician are on common ground: for it is only by the oblique methods of the artist, by the use of aesthetic suggestion and musical rhythm, that the wonder of that vision can be expressed."[4]

When I studied Organ Performance at Oberlin Conservatory of Music, there was no talk of one's religious life, spirituality, or relationship to God. On the positive side, I learned self-discipline, how to structure time, and how to focus concentration. I also learned about history firsthand, about architecture and instruments, styles and performance practices, conventions and fads. I read treatises and manuals, listened to recordings of music, studied and analyzed scores, and trained my ears to distinguish intervals and take rhythmic, melodic, and harmonic dictation. The goal was to play the organ to the best of my ability.

On the negative side, the pressure to spend more time than anyone else in the practice room was constant. Two hours a day was paltry; eight hours of practice a day was worth bragging about. I also discovered that the difficulty of performing on a musical instrument involved more than technique and musicianship. The more I learned, the more I realized I did not know, and the easier it was for insecurity and doubt to plague my practice time. Competition with other students was not a strong enough motivation for me to play as well as I could. It seemed as if every time I began to play well and complimented myself, I immediately made a mistake. Perfection as a goal drained all the joy out of performing. Memorizing music required a level of concentration and self-confidence that was new to me. Why was I playing, and what was I trying to say? Was it all just for attention, to be in the spotlight and receive applause? If so, the audience applause never seemed enough to merit the endless hours of practice. And the congregation often was not listening.

When I graduated from Oberlin and went to Europe to study, however, my quest to understand my role as a musician had only begun. I had conquered many of my fears and doubts with increased skills and competence, but the questions remained: Why was I playing, and what was I trying to say? I began to discover that I was inspired not only when playing superb instruments, but also by the holiness of the building, of the space in which I played. Every recital had the feel of a battle. I had to get myself in shape — physically, emotionally, mentally, and spiritually — in order to move through the voices that would negate my music making, that tried to rob me of the joy I know when my soul connects directly through my fingers and feet and speaks to God. I became hungry for this transcendent conversation. I was more comfortable claiming this part of my identity in church than in the recital hall, but I discovered that my playing, no matter where I was, directly connected to my relationship with the Divine. I could no longer deny this.

It was at Harvard Divinity School, years after I had completed all the required memorized recitals for master's and doctoral degrees, that I came across Athanasius's fourth-century biography of Antony, one of the first Christian ascetics, considered to be the "Father of all monks."[5] Monasticism, which is rooted in ascetic practice,[6] became popular after Christianity was

legalized and the threat of martyrdom no longer pro-
vided the motivation to sharpen one's faith. Richard
Valantasis, a scholar and Episcopal priest, defines asceticism as "performances designed to inaugurate an
alternative culture, to enable different social relations,
and to create a new identity."[7] These spiritual performances (such as "fasting, withdrawal from society,
silence, physical prayer, and manual labor") were employed as a way to purify the soul and "live as an
angel."[8] Athanasius described Antony's regimen of self-
discipline and self-scrutiny as involving warfare with
Satan's forces. Even in isolation, Antony spoke of being
crowded with demons.

> *What was missing from my
> training was a deliberate connection
> between my music making and my
> spirituality.*

As we struggled with this strange material, I began
to realize that it was not at all foreign to me. Here
was an answer to what I had been seeking. Musical
performance is an ascetic discipline. The description
of Antony's demons was totally familiar; the way they
talk and pretend to speak like the devout, the way they
try to cause confusion and create disturbances. Here is
a perfect description of what goes on in the head of

the performer during the first ten minutes of a recital, the settling-down time before one is able to give one-self over completely to the music. What was missing from my training was a deliberate connection between my music making and my spirituality. No one had ever encouraged me as a musician to articulate my relation-ship with God and to acknowledge that this is at the core of everything that I do. Once I understood that connection, the spiritual warfare made sense and was inevitable. I could then claim the solution that both Athanasius and Antony had discovered: prayer, self-discipline, and praising God in music send the demons scurrying away, align our relationship with the Divine, and enable us to feel joy.

Howard Gardner, in *Intelligence Reframed: Multiple Intelligences for the Twenty-First Century*, has changed the way society thinks about creativity and intel-ligence.[9] After years of research with children and brain-damaged adults, Gardner discovered that "people have a wide range of capacities,"[10] and that linguis-tic and logical-mathematical intelligences, traditionally tested on exams such as Scholastic Aptitude Tests, do not represent the full capacity of intelligences of which the human brain is capable. Not only did Gard-ner come to the conclusion that musical intelligence had been left out, but he came up with a number of other intelligences, including bodily-kinesthetic, spa-tial, interpersonal, intrapersonal, and naturalist.[11] He even discusses the possibility of existential and spiritual intelligences.[12]

At divinity school I discovered the truth of these different ways of knowing. Everything about the school seemed designed to increase linguistic and logical-mathematical skills through hefty, difficult readings, written assignments and exams, intense conversations, seminars, and language study. Additionally, interpersonal and intrapersonal intelligences were developed if one took field education and clinical pastoral education. However, there was only one professor who offered courses with academic standing that developed any form of artistic intelligence.[13] Where were music and the arts? Students were expected to be able to sing hymns in chapel but were never taught basic musical skills. Generally speaking, we were taught how to write but not how to draw, how to read but not how to see, how to speak but not how to listen. Without the lively arts to inspire us, irritate us, and prophesy to us, something critically important to theological education was missing — the expectation that a living God still speaks today to God's people, that the Holy Spirit continues to move and breathe on us. How can we train ministers to hear God's voice in the world if we do not know how to listen?

You, the sacred musician, connect us to another part of our brain, to a part of ourselves that we might otherwise neglect and ignore. We need to sing, and we need to engage our entire body in the act of worship. We long to be part of something bigger than ourselves. You are one of our guides.

Being a guide to our conversation with the Almighty may be a more profound role than you bargained for. Your spiritual state becomes not just important, but critical. What can sacred musicians do to prepare themselves more fully for this awesome task?

In my own life, an important breakthrough occurred when I sought out a spiritual director. A spiritual director is someone grounded in prayer, serious about his or her own religious life, and wise in the ways of the Spirit. After you have dealt with life's anger and disappointments through therapy or counseling and have reached some level of acceptance and maturity, you may find yourself seeking a different form of guidance.

A spiritual director helps you process your life through the lens of your relationship with God. In this context you will begin to discover your own belief system and whether or not your views of the Almighty are truly divine. Often we discover that we have allowed voices that are not holy to have power over us. This process of discovery is called discernment: the ability to distinguish between good and evil. Actually, when you think about it, why on earth would a church musician have a spiritual director? It is much easier to write about why sacred musicians would *not* want to do this. The process could actually be very disruptive to your life and would probably change everything, including every relationship that you have. So here are forty-five reasons why a musician in a religious institution would definitely *not* want to find a good spiritual director:

1. You would have to accept the fact that God made you and that you are good.

2. You would have to believe that God might have use of you.

3. You would have to accept that earth is not heaven, that spiritual forces of good *and* evil are at play in the world around you.

4. You would have to accept that in this daily spiritual warfare, evil will try to infiltrate wherever God is, particularly in religious institutions.

5. You would have to discern whether you value working for good or for evil.

6. You would have to be upset when you realize that evil succeeded in "pushing your buttons," and that you have just done Satan's bidding.

7. You would have to look at your entire existence with "other eyes."

8. You would have to let go of your life's store of anger, self-pity, and self-hatred.

9. You would have to let go of your worldly ambitions for fame, wealth, and adulation and pray to understand God's will for you.

10. You would have to examine your motives carefully and accept that they are not always pure.

11. You would have to accept the fact that you are not a perfect human being.

12. You would have to be willing to admit that you make mistakes, that you sin.

13. You would have to learn to ask forgiveness from God and from people whom you have hurt.

14. You would have to learn to laugh at yourself.

15. You would have to learn to ask for help.

16. You would have to begin to look at people whom you have rejected as worthless or "below you" with new eyes, *even people who sing out of tune.*

17. You would have to seek out those with whom you are angry and talk to them.

18. You would have to admit that community is important and find ways to spend time with people who love God.

19. You would have to give up gossip and stop looking for other people's flaws.

20. You would have to give up destructive addictions.

21. You would have to rejoice in other people's successes.

22. You would have to learn to love without hooks.

23. You would have to learn how to play your instrument or conduct your choir knowing that you stand in the presence of the Divine One — every time.

24. You would have to learn to give your art away — to truly offer it to God and not do it just for applause or a pat on the back.

25. You would have to give up trying to make a beautiful musical line by screaming at your choir in rehearsal.

26. You would have to learn kinder, gentler techniques.

27. You would have to learn to be compassionate, generous, and humble.

28. You would have to learn to see other people as separate from yourself and not as a reflection of you — to see God in them.

29. You would have to be kind to your minister, and maybe even offer him or her suggestions about how to do ministry better without turning it into an insult.

30. You would have to pray with your clergyperson.

31. You would have to ask for suggestions on how to do your job better.

32. You would have to stop talking destructively about clergy and other musicians behind their backs.

33. You would have to figure out how to ask for a raise because it is the right and just thing for the position, not just because of insecurities about your self-worth.

34. You would have to work on healing your wounds.

35. You would have to care whether your music making inspires the congregation and seek to change it if it does not.

36. You would have to adjust your music program in some way that reflects awareness of the spirituality of the community in which you are working.

37. You would have to allow your choir to grow spiritually and choose music that will aid them in this process.

38. You would have to grow musically, emotionally, and spiritually.

39. You would have to pray.

40. You would have to add time in your busy schedule for meditation and Bible reading.

41. You would have to add spiritual books to your reading list.

42. You would have to confront your fear of death and accept that your time on earth is limited.

43. Rather than avoid those you know with terminal diseases, you would have to seek them out for their gifts of presence and insight.

44. You would have to "waste time" with God.

45. You would have to be the best musician that you can *and* give yourself over to God.

All in all, I think that it is much easier not to open this can of worms. God only knows where it might lead.

Four

THE GIFT OF DIVERSITY

A Doonesbury cartoon dating from the early 1990s: The minister is sitting in an empty church talking to his old friend. "It's an interesting congregation, Mike. Members are far more consumer conscious than they used to be. The church has to **deliver** for its members! Counseling, social events, recovery programs, tutoring, fitness center — we have to offer it all!"

Mike answers, "Where's God fit into all this?"

"God? Well, God's still the draw for sure. He's got the big name."

"But do you ever evoke it anymore?"

"Um . . . Frankly, Mike, God comes with a lot of baggage, the whole male, eurocentric guilt thing."*

This is a difficult and confusing time for ministry in religious institutions. Both conservatives and liberals are struggling to discern whether politically correct statements are "in" or "out." Are we for or against diversity? What about our own heritage and identity? As church and synagogue musicians, we know that many people are drawn to religious services because of the music, and yet, even in Garry Trudeau's insightful cartoon, God *and* music have been left out of the conversation about parish programming in favor of more fashionable goods and services. Where exactly is music ministry located in the current prioritization of religious institutions? And where is God in all of this?

In the summer of 1991, as part of my preparation for ordination to the priesthood, I took Clinical Pastoral Education (CPE), field education in a hospital setting. I thought I was going to be taught how to do chaplaincy work. I quickly discovered that the program was not directly concerned with teaching us how to help others, but was designed as a catalyst for self-discovery and discernment, pushing every button that exists concerning illness, death and dying, as well as group dynamics. We were forced to look in depth at our own woundedness, pain, and prejudices. What a summer!

The group that I worked with could not have been more diverse. We were from the United States, Africa, and India; we were Jewish, Episcopalian, Catholic, Unitarian-Universalist, Seventh-day Adventist, United Methodist, and African Methodist Episcopal Zion; we were ordained, working toward ordination, living a monastic life, and struggling with religious identity. We were young and old, heterosexual and homosexual, with and without children, and with and without committed relationships. Our naïve delight in the surprising extent of our diversity did not last for very long.

We were each responsible for organizing services on different days. There was an initial excitement about sharing worship with each other. This wore off very quickly, as we discovered how difficult and painful worshiping together actually was. Music and readings that made some people ecstatically happy drove others out of the chapel, choking back tears and profound feelings of rejection. The words of our different traditions got in the way of worshiping together, as did different musical styles. We discovered that every liturgical decision had its limitations, with different advocates and detractors. As hard as we tried, no single liturgy worked for everyone. Finally, the only way that we could worship together was silence — great long periods of meditation. Here we were in agreement. It was only in silence that we could feel the presence of God in our midst.

A new complaint arose. The summer was almost over, and we had not experienced each other's traditions. We had been so obsessed with trying to convert each other that we had not been present to each other's way of worshiping. We had not been interested in getting to know each other.

With great trepidation, I announced that on Friday morning I would be leading a traditional Episcopal Rite II Service of Morning Prayer, complete with all of the strengths and weaknesses of the 1979 Book of Common Prayer. "Feel free not to come," I announced.

Much to my surprise, everyone showed up. As we sang and prayed together, I cried. Because of our previous detailed arguments and discussions, I had a good idea of what everyone was thinking and feeling at various places in the service — which passages were particularly painful, and at which points certain colleagues would need to remain silent in order to be true to themselves. I was profoundly moved that they had come anyway, despite the differences, and that they were sharing a way of worship, as imperfect as it was, that had become important to me.

Something was holding us together, some bond that rose above words and music. We had argued ferociously because we cared about each other, and yet we did not know how to state our own beliefs without hurting each other. We were learning to accept the fact that none of us had all of the answers, but that together, as a group, it seemed as though we had some of them. In short, we had become a congregation.

We also learned that there was no need to try to convert each other. God did not need our pitiful attempts at getting others to experience life the way we do. How presumptuous and arrogant of us. We learned to feel awe and respect for each other because we began to understand that each of us, no matter what our mode of expression, was trying to worship God.

God is the most important figure in the liturgy. The Spirit hovers above the tension between word and music, between verbal and non-verbal, between the certainty of a belief system and the uncertainty of crisis-time doubts. Here is our failing: we do not really want God to be in charge. We want that power. We want life to be consistent, predictable, and controllable. We want other people to be just like us, to behave like us, and to worship like us. This belief system is prevalent in our society, and it is profoundly flawed because it denies the hugeness and variety of creation. Making ourselves the center of the universe is idolatry.

The only way to move away from this narcissism is to embrace the variety of creation. Diversity is one of the greatest gifts we have been given. Trips to foreign countries reveal the immense variety of animal and plant life on earth, let alone peoples, languages, and cultures. Our own communities reflect this diversity in ethnic restaurants, stores, and festive celebrations. We would feel impoverished if there were no new things to discover — no new songs, new compositions, new art, new plays, new shows, new movies, new cartoons, new foods. We would get bored. Our lives are enriched by exploration, innovation, and revelation. This is how we grow.

Here is also where it gets really difficult, however. This is where our artistic integrity conflicts with pastoral concerns. In my own life, this is where Dr. Victoria Sirota, recitalist and highly accomplished musician, struggles with Mother Vicki, an inner-city priest. Mother Vicki wants to include everybody and never leave anyone out. Dr. Sirota is a perfectionist with the highest musical standards who rejoices in carefully planned and executed services with superb musicians and sensitively chosen repertoire. Mother Vicki delights in a comfortable chaos in which anything can happen during the liturgy. How can these two opposing views be reconciled?

We want other people to be just like us, to behave like us, and to worship like us.

There is no easy answer. The tension will always be there — believe me, I know! Both sides present a valid truth in their own way. The struggle is to understand the importance of this particular dialectic: on the one hand, a highly formal liturgy with music performed at its absolute best with careful attention to detail and time constraints; on the other hand, a more informal liturgy where spontaneity is prized above precision and there is less concern about beginning and ending on time. Both forms of liturgy can provide very moving worship experiences. An extreme of either form of liturgy is problematic, however, because we end up worshiping the form instead of the Living One. This idolatry may occur in a "high" liturgy when time constraints have become too important, or the service is too perfectly performed and no longer felt (this reveals itself by the amount of yelling that goes on in the sacristy to get people, especially children, to behave properly). The idolatry of an informal "low" liturgy may occur when the congregation is held hostage by sloppy planning, poor execution, and the lack of any time constraints. Whether notated or improvised, familiar or new, music can lead us beyond ourselves into holy space. To live in the balance between the tensions of competing musics and liturgical styles is to be aware of one's own prejudices and more open to the voice of God.

Viewing diversity as a gift helps us get our theology right, teaches us humility in the face of otherness, and evokes awe in the presence of the Creator. It has a huge impact on the choice of music for our worship. The openness of the music program to a variety of genres, styles, and spiritualities does greater honor to God's creation. Embracing the congregation lovingly with a larger variety of different sounds balancing the new and daring with the familiar and comfortable also keeps the assembly in a posture more open to divine revelation. The signal sent to anyone who walks in the door is that, in truth, all are welcome. When this happens, the music program is not only important, but it has become essential to living out a theology that is a true manifestation of God's love. Counseling, social events, recovery pro-grams, tutoring, and fitness centers are well and good, but the real purpose of a worshiping community is to worship God. Great liturgical moments open our hearts and minds to much deeper truths about ourselves, the world around us, and our relationship with God. This is the conversation for which we hunger.

Five

SILENCE

But the Lord is in his holy temple; let all the earth keep silence before him! (Hab. 2:20)

WHY TALK ABOUT silence in a book for musicians? It does not make sense. We are the ones who fill the sanctuary with sounds, all different kinds of sounds depending on the mood we are setting. We may use extra trumpets and timpani on a feast day, or have our choir sing *a cappella* on a day of atonement. Why speak of silence? Because it is the quality of the silence surrounding the music that helps the music lift off the ground.

There is a difference in the silence before and after a musical offering. Before, the air is charged with expectation. What will we hear? After, if the music making has been inspired, the echoes of the music linger in the air like incense and carry us heavenward. This is one of those liminal moments when heaven and earth meet. We have been used by the Divine, and we stand on holy ground: "...the Lord is in his holy temple; let all the earth keep silence before him!"

Many services of worship are held with time constraints. One service follows quickly after another one, or there is Sunday School or an adult education forum. A reason can always be found to justify rushing through the words, picking a faster tempo, and eliminating all silence. The only problem with this approach is that people leave the service more exhausted than when they came. Rather than being nourished, they are out of breath.

Organists are sometimes asked to cover silence, as if silence is a great mistake in worship. "Quick, play something!" we are told when some minor mishap results in an unanticipated pause. Why not sit in silence for a few minutes? What are we afraid of?

> *God has all the time in the world.*

The Greeks have two different words for time: *chronos*, chronological time as defined by the clock, and *kairos*, God's eternal time. When a service is being run by the clock, everyone can feel it. There is a tension in the air. The congregant cannot relax into God's holy presence. Worship becomes a series of accomplishments, a "to do" list with items checked off. The big question is, "Did we end on time?"

This is actually worshiping the clock. (Is there a word for that — chronosólatry?) Of course it is appropriate to pay attention to how long things take, but consider those instances when worship leaders have actually given over their power and ability for creating truly sacred space to the bullying voice that does not actually want to be there in the first place. Remember, Satan is always in a hurry. God has all the time in the world.

Just because you have the physical constraint of a one-hour service does not mean that you cannot encourage the feeling of *kairos* time at some point in the service. Silence can do this more effectively than anything. Discuss with your minister the possibility of allowing a full minute of silence to contemplate the scripture. Tell people that you are experimenting with this to bring the worship to a different place. Let everyone get used to the idea over time. Let them settle into it. Or when the choir has moved to their places before an anthem, wait a moment with heads bowed. Take a deep breath, and then begin. The sound will change immediately. And at the end, do not break the silence so quickly. A few extra seconds may make an incredible difference.

Obviously, if you add silence around every event, your service will end up much too long. Figure out one thing to cut or shorten. The congregation will need to get used to the presence of silence in the service, but will be grateful for the gift once they have learned how to receive it. Be kind to them, and especially gentle with children. Asking children to think about God with their eyes closed might end up providing the best natural material for a children's sermon.

In order to feel God's presence, we need to stop the clock, step outside of our busy lives, and sit in hushed quietude. Even time needs to stand still. "The Lord is in his holy temple. Let all the earth keep silence before him."

Six

COMPOSERS AS PROPHETS

I N HIS FIRST Charles Eliot Norton Lecture at Harvard University, Aaron Copland stated: "An unusual and disturbing situation has gradually become all-pervasive at public performances of music: the universal preponderance of old music on concert programs."[1] He goes on to suggest that this unhealthy phenomenon "tends to make all music listening safe and unadventurous since it deals so largely in the works of the accepted masters."[2] Copland points out that concerts across the world are exact replicas of each other. He surmises, "Music is no longer merely an international language, it is an international commodity."[3]

It is disheartening to realize that Copland spoke those words over fifty years ago. Our infatuation with the past hinders our ability to live fully in the present. In contrast to the twenty-first century, composers in the more distant past were always encouraged to write new music. The audience of three hundred years ago was more like the audience of a fashion show — no one was interested in last year's effort. Vivaldi would probably be mortified to find out that we listen to *all* of his music and easily hear when he repeats himself. With records and radio, CDs and MP3 players, we all can choose our favorite "master" and stick with that music — which by now has become safe and predictable. Haydn's *Surprise Symphony* holds no surprise; Beethoven's Fifth is programmed so often that any audience could probably sing it.

We are fearful of contemporary music. Few of us personally know a living composer. Can you imagine living in Bach's time and never bothering to step into his church? We might have said something like, "Well, I only listen to Palestrina." What a shame to miss the opportunity to be one of the early supporters and fans of such a great soul before his music was given the stamp of universal approval.

Composers today must compete not only with their contemporaries, but also with the best composers from centuries past. Copland writes, "Reverence for the classics in our time has been turned into a form of discrimination against all other music."[4] The good news is that more music is being listened to than ever before. The bad news is that it has become even more difficult for living composers to find their place in our society. We seem to prefer them dead.

One of the most significant contributions of the American Guild of Organists (AGO) has been the commissioning of new compositions for regional and national conventions, the source of great joy and excitement at every convention I've ever attended. These include new works by Leslie Adams, William Albright, Milton Babbitt, Robert Harris, Walter Hilse, Libby Larson, Dan Locklair, Dorothy Papadakos, Stephen Paulus, McNeil Robinson, Gunther Schuller, Konrad Susa, and Ellen Taaffe Zwilich, among others. We have acted as patrons of our discipline and helped in the birthing process of new repertoire. What makes it thrilling is that we do not always know if we will like it. We cannot control the creation, only pray it into existence. The act of commissioning a work is adventurous. Now we, the performers and listeners, play an important role in helping to determine if this is a great piece or if it is mediocre.

Copland posits, "A masterwork awakens in us reactions of a spiritual order that are already in us, only waiting to be aroused."[5] Not only do we as listeners find the work interesting, but we are brought to a place familiar to us where truths reside. The music itself changes what we are thinking about. Copland refers to a musical performance as "a reincarnation of a series of ideas implicit in the work of art."[6] Through listening to a masterwork, we are moved from the trivial and mundane to the profound.

Therefore the questions we ask when listening to a new work include: Does the piece engage us, does it hold our interest? Does the composer write well for the organ, does he or she show potential as an organ composer, or is his or her style better suited to another medium? What is the composer trying to say to us, and does it awaken "a spiritual order" that is already in us?

On July 6, 2000, among the new works that we heard at the Seattle National AGO Convention was the premiere of Robert Sirota's concerto for organ and orchestra, *In the Fullness of Time*. Hatsumi Miura performed the piece on a magnificent new Fisk instrument in the new Benaroya Hall with the Seattle Symphony Orchestra. Why was I so excited about this premiere? Well, obviously in part because it is my husband's composition. But also because despite my familiarity with it, I did not know exactly what it would sound like.

> *The danger in performing music only by dead composers is ultimately a theological one.*

I had seen the score, indeed I heard the composer wrestling it into creation. I know that he hears it as a huge ceiling fresco. *In the Fullness of Time* is a vision of the end time, the second coming. The title is derived from Eucharistic Prayer B in the Book of Common Prayer.[7] I had helped the process by playing through the organ part looking for mistakes and had enjoyed its new sonorities and melodies. I had also heard a tape of a rehearsal with a downsized version of orchestra and organ.

But what would the piece sound like with a huge instrument and orchestra in a magnificent space? Would it grab the listeners and lift us to a higher plane? I first began commissioning my husband to compose organ music (an organ concerto for my senior recital at Oberlin Conservatory of Music) a year after we were married. That piece has since been pulled from his corpus, as has the solo organ work that I premiered in Paris the next year, dedicated to André Marchal. Robert Sirota's catalogue now includes numerous pieces for organ, for organ and another instrument, two organ concertos, and a number of choral works with organ, including a Mass.

The reason for writing this is not really to advertise the organ music of Robert Sirota (although I would rejoice if more people played his music), but to share with you what it has meant to me as a performer to work with a living composer. First of all, it is difficult. The music talks back. Let me explain. When I am learning a new piece, I make decisions about how I think it should be played. Often, however, my information is incomplete, and my editorializing (slight change of tempo, addition of rubato, change of registration, etc.) may actually skew the architecture. Over the last thirty-five years, I have learned how to work on a new Sirota composition with care and humility. I am still anxious before playing it for the composer, even though I know him well. I am often surprised by his response. Some decisions of which I have been uncertain, he has been delighted with. Others to which I feel a strong commitment, he has disagreed with. I have learned how my husband hears his music and have a much better idea of what he wants. Bob, in the meantime, has learned how to write idiomatic music that is more easily accessible, yet still remains faithful to his compositional style and sound world.

The surprise from this complicated relationship of performer and composer is that it has changed how I look at the music of dead composers. Yes, it is easier to play their music because it does not talk back. But this does not mean that any decision I make is a good one, that putting the stamp of my own personality on it is not a distortion of what was intended. There is a wonderful Animaniacs cartoon in which the concert pianist, looking amazingly like Lorin Hollander (and actually drawn by Lorin's brother Nicholas, I discovered!) prefaces his performance of Schubert's *Sonata in A major* by saying something like, "I am now going to play this piece not as the composer wrote it, but as he intended it!"[8]

As performers, it is easy to become arrogant, thinking that we know what is best for a composition. This is why studying different performance practices, checking original manuscripts and editions, taking lessons with people who have studied with the composer or the student of that composer, or listening to old recordings can be invaluable tools to allowing the music to "talk back." And living composers delight in answering questions about their music. I assure you the great majority would love to know that you care. Pick up the phone and ask them your question. This might even lead to you or your organization commissioning them for a next piece. We need to maintain a healthy respect for the complete act of creation. Otherwise we performers have become parasites.

The danger in performing music only by dead composers is ultimately a theological one. Playing the same old hymns, service music, preludes, and postludes fuels the belief that God is dead, that the Spirit is no longer active. We are basically proclaiming that our Creator has finally abandoned us. The *New York Times* keeps mentioning the same few "approved of" living composers over and over again, and because they are aging, then proclaims that the world of musical theatre, orchestral music, opera, etc., etc., is dying out. Not so. There are wonderful composers, young and old, just waiting to be discovered. The Spirit is alive and well, and God keeps inspiring our artists with new ideas and new creations. You do not have to marry a composer to share this experience. Have the courage to nurture a living composer and watch what happens.

How did the performance of *In the Fullness of Time* go? Miura played exquisitely, the Seattle Symphony under Gerard Schwarz was superb, and the performance was hair-raising. How did the piece fare? The Seattle Symphony reprogrammed it for the next year's subscription series and called Miura back from Japan to play it again. Professor David Boe performed it at the installation of the new Fisk organ at Finney Chapel at Oberlin College, and I played it on a new Bedient organ with the Lincoln Symphony Orchestra (Nebraska) under Edward Polochick for their Seventy-fifth Anniversary Concert. The most recent performance was in Meridian, Mississippi. In addition, Michael Barone recorded it at the Seattle Convention and included it in one of his *Pipedreams* national broadcasts from Minnesota Public Radio. The way to encourage new music is to keep playing it, keep listening to it, and to keep commissioning more pieces from composers whose music you like.

By the end of Johann Sebastian Bach's life, his music was considered outdated, too scholarly and esoteric. The Rococo period, which overlapped the end of the Baroque era, featured music that was easier to comprehend quickly, with far fewer notes. Imagine Bach's frustration and sadness thinking that his life's work had become passé. Bach, like any other composer or artist, must have been tempted continually not to be Bach — to stop composing, to go to the tavern to drown his sorrows and escape the cacophony of a house full of children, musicians who were less than perfect, a difficult and demanding work situation, and constant monetary troubles. But instead he allowed his trials to bring him closer to God. In gratitude, he wrote page after page of divine polyphony, generously sharing his faith, hope, and inspiration with people like us, people he would never know.

The act of composition is a communal effort. It requires a relationship between composer, muse, performer, and listener. Performers and listeners play an active role. Our encouragement and nurture of the creative voice benefits not just the composer. Our world is enlarged as we contribute to this divine conversation.

Seven

GROUND ZERO

THIS IS MY THIRD VISIT to New York City since September 11 and the first time I have had courage to pay my respects. The avoidance of it was beginning to hang heavily on me.

Ground Zero is still a shock, a massive pile of rubble with only an echo of Yamasaki's Gothic windows, the eerie brightness of unfettered sunlight, the omnipresence of policemen and firemen, demolition and construction workers, police barricades, green mesh fences obstructing the view, makeshift shrines, fresh flowers and dead ones from earlier heartfelt tributes, the faces of missing loved ones staring from scattered posters, walls of written messages by well-wishers from all over the world, signs urging visitors not to video or take pictures ("This means you!"), various vistas where pilgrims stand in awed silence, unable to comprehend how any human being could willingly do this to another, hushed conversation and tears, the stench of death still hanging in the air in late November 2001. There is concrete debris in the air. My throat feels sore. I find I cannot cry, and I cannot stand still. A vague nausea has me wondering if I will ever feel hungry again. So I keep moving, trying to grasp the magnitude of the destruction by walking its perimeter.

I am surprised to come upon St. Paul's Chapel, dating from 1766 and miraculously standing despite its proximity to the World Trade Center. Now it has become a place of physical, mental, and spiritual nurture for relief workers, some sitting wearily on the steps. God only knows what their eyes have seen today. My disappointment that St. Paul's is closed to the public makes me realize that I am seeking something, some tangible solace, some place of respite in the midst of this din, some holy ground.

With the first sight of Trinity Church on Broadway at Wall Street, my heart leaps. There it is, the magnificent Upjohn building dating from 1846 unscathed and reasserting itself as a dominant architectural presence. I duck inside as the altar is being censed, the priest then saying, "The Lord be with you" and the congregation responding, "And also with you." Never has Richard Proulx's *Sanctus* sounded so magnificent, and never have I felt so strongly the presence of angelic choirs, saints, and martyrs surrounding and consoling us. The incense mixes earthly pain with heavenly compassion. The electronic organ and keyboard with speakers in the back balcony that replace the now-silenced Aeolian Skinner works surprisingly well, the sound benefiting from the lively acoustics and the gifted touch of a fine musician.

And then we are called up to the altar, strangers quickly becoming community, disparate souls partaking of Christ's body and blood. The violence of Christ's crucifixion speaks to me in a new way. This One who knows terror and evil better than we do comforts us. The tears flow easily. The outrageous intimacy of the Eucharistic Feast, especially in such a place at such a time, calms, restores, and blesses.

At the end of the service, a chance meeting with a dear sister of the Society of Saint Margaret results in a longed-for embrace and the opportunity to shower love on one who ministers here. This time I see the familiar wooden cross that Sister Marjorie Raphael wears as a visual reassurance that God has called good souls to be present here. The celebrant, an African American priest with a voice of great power, responds to my gratitude. We discover a mutual Baltimore friend. I find out that the weekday Eucharists have been reinstituted only a few days prior due to the massive cleanup that the sanctuary required. I hear distant music and seek it out. The gift shop is playing a wonderful new Christmas recording of the Choir of Trinity Church, conducted by Owen Burdick. And there are the joyful sounds of the pipe organ. I buy the recording while blessing the memory of Larry King, who had graciously allowed me to play it in a summer organ series in 1974.

Fortified more deeply, I return to the sidewalk and continue walking south and west until I am forced to turn back. But as I return, this time I notice the signs of life, the restaurants, cafés, and bars reopening, the jubilant notices clamoring for attention, New Yorkers dressed in business attire and speaking on cell phones as they gingerly step across boards and puddles. The city is coming back to life.

> *It is easy to feel that evil is winning.*

Minuro Yamasaki, the chief architect of the World Trade Center, stated in 1976, "The World Trade Center is a living symbol of man's dedication to world peace ... beyond the compelling need to make this a monument to world peace, the World Trade Center should, because of its importance, become a representation of man's belief in humanity, his need for individual dignity, his belief in the cooperation of men, and through cooperation, his ability to find greatness."[1] Following the service at Trinity, the sister said, "September 11 makes us one with the world. They didn't think we ever suffer. Now we share suffering with the rest of the world."

Our world has changed since September 11, 2001. Many of you were called to play, sing, and conduct at extra services, funerals, memorial services, and concerts in honor of the victims. Again and again I have heard how freely and profoundly you offered your artistic gifts. You comforted those who mourned and embraced the world with God's love. Your healing presence in this broken world is crucial.

It is easy to feel that evil is winning. An empty place at a family table becomes particularly poignant during the holiday season. There are many more people grieving, many who have been helping in the aftermath of tragedy and many the world over who are so horrified that they feel the losses in the pit of their stomach. We have smelled the smoke and stench of death. Is there hope for the world?

You remain a primary caregiver to the average person. And because so many more people flock to our religious institutions in times of crisis, you feel the increased pressure to do a great job. You are on the frontline. You are there whether the disaster is manmade or natural — a car accident, hijacking, bombing, tsunami, hurricane, or earthquake. With your music you greet the survivors, the relatives, the friends, and the newly homeless; you comfort those who have lost everything and those who are grieving; you bless those who are in pain and suffering and those who are dying. You are also there when the crisis is not as dramatic, but the loss as profound. Remember that God asks that you be faithful, not perfect. Much will happen that is outside of your control. Please take extra care of yourself physically, emotionally, and spiritually. We need your joy and hope. Remember also that God delights in you. And don't forget to laugh.

May the brilliant light of the Divine Mystery banish all darkness in the days and weeks to come.

> *Please Lord, I pray for peace:*
> *in this time of intensity,*
>> *the peace to play Your music prayerfully.*
> *in this time of desperation,*
>> *the peace to do Your work faithfully.*
> *in this time of anxiety,*
>> *the peace to lead Your people lovingly.*
> *in this time of fear,*
>> *the peace to sing Your praises hopefully.*
> *in this time of grieving,*
>> *the peace to feel compassion.*
> *in this Holy Season,*
>> *deep peace within that I may hear Your Voice.*
> *Amen.*

Eight

WORSHIP WARS
AND CONFLICT

D ONALD HUSTAD writes in his book *True Worship: Reclaiming the Wonder and Majesty*, "At a recent convention of choral directors in San Diego, delegates were discussing the worship ferment in the churches they served. 'Our church offers four different services that feature traditional, praise and worship, country, and jazz music,' said one. A not-to-be-outdone Lutheran choir director retorted, 'We have five different styles of worship, and the pastor changes his outfit for each one!' "[1]

Religious institutions as we know them are changing. The new growth movement aimed at seekers features a popular music style that can be threatening to musicians who possess a more classical musical education. This is not just happening in fundamentalist churches, but mainstream Presbyterian, Methodist, Lutheran, etc. as well.[2]

The issues raised are many. Different musical styles express different kinds of spirituality. There is no one kind of music that inspires and satisfies everyone's desires. Sometimes, however, a new style may be touted as the answer to a congregation's difficulties, often at the expense of a more traditional music program. It is hard for the faithful musician who has been working there for years not to feel this personally. The inclusion of new musical styles cannot fix everything, however, and will create new problems if not done in a sensitive and loving way.

What are these worship wars really about? In some ways, they have the feel of class warfare. The traditional music of the congregation may be seen as elitist (historic music that requires a musical education to fully appreciate). The new music may be viewed as easier to listen to and easier to sing along with — more popular. Generation gap tension also adds to the mix. Young people may wonder why they have to sing the music of their parents when they would prefer to sing their own tunes.

H. Wiley Hitchcock, in *Music in the United States: A Historical Introduction*, points out that Americans speak colloquially of "classical" and "popular" music, terms that are difficult to pin down. Hitchcock chooses instead to use the terms "cultivated" and "vernacular" traditions:

I mean by the term "cultivated tradition" a body of music that America had to cultivate consciously, music faintly exotic, to be approached with some effort, and to be appreciated for its edification, its moral, spiritual, or aesthetic values. By the "vernacular tradition" I mean a body of music more plebeian, native, not approached self-consciously but simply grown into as one grows into one's vernacular tongue; music understood and appreciated simply for its utilitarian or entertainment value.[3]

These two different musical streams, quite frankly, appeal to different people depending on background, education, cultural heritage, and spiritual journey. What we are really witnessing is the reawakening of a deep desire to be put in touch with a living God. Not the God of our grandparents or parents, but the God who understands us exactly in the culture in which *we* live and move. This hunger for the sacred is a good thing.

How we go about trying to respond to this hunger may result in conflict. Here is where our different, strongly felt views can create difficulties. Because something has worked well in the past is not a good enough reason to keep it unchanged. The corporate body is growing spiritually, and the choice of music, whether cultivated, vernacular, or a blend of the two, needs to reflect that growth. A vibrant music program that blends the familiar with well-performed new music (whether from the standard repertoire, an alternative style, or newly commissioned works) encourages the congregation, choir, clergy, and staff to keep rethinking their relationship with God. Making changes just for the sake of change, however, can destroy trusting relationships and ultimately disrupt worship.

This is a hard topic for me to discuss because as musician and priest I struggle within myself over these issues. My three music degrees encourage me to be critical of music that is not well written, or is in a style that is cheaply sentimental. Dr. Sirota has high professional standards. Her alter ego, Mother Vicki, wants to engage everyone who walks in the door and even those who are not present. Her concern is to widen the musical net so that no one is left out, so that everyone feels that their personal way of approaching God, whether cultivated or vernacular, is valued.

Agreeing to remain in this tension is a difficult thing to do. My gut instinct is to try to solve the problem. If this is probably not possible this side of heaven, then how else can we view this particular tension? Can we look at worship in a way that will honor the tradition, respect the differences inherent in the corporate body, and still invite healthy growth?

The spirituality of the gathered faithful may manifest itself in introverted or extraverted ways. In worship that features introverted spirituality, the liturgy is processed more internally. Silence matters. Spatial distance, separateness from others, is helpful to feeling God's presence. The congregant holds a more passive role in the service and enjoys listening to fine music performed by the choir and organist. There are minimal congregational responses and movement. A baby's cry is a disruption.

In worship that features extraverted spirituality, the liturgy is processed communally. Ecstatic outbursts are commonplace. The congregant is actively involved in the service, singing, clapping, yelling encouragement to the preacher, humming along with the choir anthem. There are numerous occasions throughout the service for the congregation to move around, to hug and touch each other. A baby's cry will hardly be noticed.

Inspired worship employs both kinds of spirituality. Worship that leans toward the extraverted will be all the richer if it honors an appropriate moment of silence; worship that is more introverted will be blessed by an occasional unprogrammed outburst of emotion. Authenticity is the goal. Authentic worship of any kind invites the Spirit to be present in a way that rigid adherence to a formula may actually discourage.

Congregations, clergy, and musicians each have their own history with the kinds of music and spirituality with which they are most accustomed and comfortable. Unless there is very careful discernment during the hiring process for either musician or minister, clashes are bound to occur as the newest staff member seeks to reconcile what he or she is used to with the corporate spirituality already in place. It is easy for a musician or clergyperson to be accommodating in the interview process. But saying that someone can work in any style is not the same as actually feeling comfortable and thriving in a style of worship other than the one they know the best. Probing questions in that regard would be very helpful to the employment process.

There are other differences to be aware of as well. Individuals have their own personality, and their own primary way of knowing — a basic programmed language that connects with their deepest identity. We tend to be most comfortable with people who think like we do and process life experiences similarly. The Myers-Briggs Type Indicator provides sixteen different combinations of personality preferences that go beyond whether someone is an extravert or introvert to include such things as how someone acquires or perceives information, reaches conclusions, makes decisions, and deals with the outside world.[4]

Howard Gardner's work on multiple intelligences has continued to expand our understanding of how different we are by pointing out that different kinds of people possess very different kinds of intelligences. Traditional IQ and standardized tests measure mostly linguistic intelligence (used by lawyers and speakers), and logical-mathematical intelligence (mathematicians and scientists).[5] Gardner questions why music has been called a talent in the past, and not another form of intelligence.[6] He adds music to the list of intelligences as well as bodily-kinesthetic (possessed by dancers and athletes), spatial (navigators and architects), interpersonal (salespeople and actors), and intrapersonal intelligences.[7]

I believe that the tension between ministers and musicians, because they tend to represent different kinds of personalities and intelligences, is almost inevitable. A musician lacking linguistic intelligence will struggle to communicate with a preacher who lacks musical intelligence. Their primary ways of knowing differ. They will have difficulty trusting each other because they do not trust a different form of expression and interpretation. Unless they choose to work on their relationship, a huge rift may occur. Remember, however, that the best, most transcendent worship will appeal to people of different personality and intelligence types. Great worship inspires the fullness of who we are — heart, mind, and soul. The respect that the minister and musician can learn to have for each other despite their differences — their ability to serve each other for the greater good — is an excellent model for a congregation. Here is servant leadership at its best.

The Apostle Paul reminds us that the corporate body is made up of different personalities and intelligences when he writes, "For as in one body we have many members, and not all the members have the same function, so we, who are many, are one body in Christ, and individually we are members one of another. We have gifts that differ according to the grace given to us" (Rom. 12:4–6).[8] With these words, Paul gathers the Roman community together, reminding them that their differences are God-given and encouraging them to respect each other's vocation.

In *Living with Contradiction*, a book of spiritual meditations on the Benedictine rule, Esther de Waal uses the architecture of a Gothic cathedral as an example of "the Pauline analogy of the body of Christ spelt out in stone."[9] She continues, "Here is never-ending conflict. The high vaults strive to push the walls outwards; the flying buttresses strive to push them inwards. Here are columns, arches, walls all locked in unceasing combat. This great cathedral is maintained, and has been maintained for centuries, through the interplay and interdependence of contradictory forces, the unremitting pull of opposites."[10] Honoring the mystery of ourselves and of each other allows us to view the tension of difference in a creative and wondrous way.

In addition to differences in personality type and intelligence, particular situations may fuel the conflict between ordained minister and musician: for new clergy, the coalition that has grown up around an established musician, and for the musician, decisions to change the musical style in the liturgy.

If the musician has been in place for years and years, he or she will have built up a following in the congregation. This is especially the case if there are successful volunteer choirs. As one of the primary lay leaders, the long-term musician has probably learned good management and pastoral skills dealing with this complex group of people who bring more than just their voices to rehearsal. It would be hard for a new clergyperson not to feel threatened by the musician's leadership, popularity, pastoral role, and even support system.

One of the recent tensions that sacred musicians have been worrying and complaining about is a clergy-based decision to change the musical style of a congregation without consulting the current musician. A well-intentioned decision may stem from the desire that the worship appeal to more young people or to a broader mix of people, or the hope that a new musical vocabulary may increase pledges. It is important to realize that a change in the corporate spirituality of a religious institution is a huge shift and needs to be processed carefully so that it does not result in splitting the congregation apart and creating new problems. If this kind of change is being contemplated, religious leaders may find the following questions helpful:

1. What is the liturgical background of the musician?

2. What is the liturgical background of the minister?

3. What is the liturgical background of the congregation?

4. Are these backgrounds similar or different? If they are different, has there been any attempt to discuss the different formations and the gifts of each?

5. Where does the idea for a change in musical style come from?

    (a) Does it come from the minister's need for worship to feel the same as it was in his or her last parish?

    (b) Is this change being used as a way to pander to or counter someone or a group of people (clergy, staff, musicians, laity, etc.) who selfishly want their own way?

    (c) Does it come from a general dissatisfaction with the repertoire choices made by the current musician and an inability to communicate that in a constructive way?

    (d) Does it arise from an unspoken tension between the musician and minister, perhaps even the minister's jealousy of the following that the musician has?

    (e) Does it come from a fear that the following the musician has is unhealthy to the spiritual growth of the community? If so, has this ever been discussed with the musician in an honest way?

> (f) Does it arise from a genuine interest on the part of the congregation to embrace new worship styles?
>
> (g) Is this change being used as a way to precipitate the departure of the musician?

6. If the hope is to increase the number of pledges, what happens if the older and wealthier congregants are angered or scared off by the new approach?

7. If the congregation sincerely wants to try something new and the clergyperson is responding to that desire, shouldn't the musician be involved in the discussion, particularly if it means changing the music program?

8. Has the musician been involved in this conversation in a way that feels supportive of his or her good work done in the past, or is this new conversation being used solely as a way to criticize the current program?

9. Is there a written contract between musician and religious institution? Does it address this kind of issue?

10. Were the liturgical concerns of the religious institution made clear when the musician was hired?

11. Is there a clear evaluation process in place for the musician that includes regular written reviews?

12. Do the musician and clergyperson meet regularly to discuss the worship — what has worked well, what didn't, and what changes might be needed by the congregation?

If the desire for a change in musical styles is being used as a way to get the musician to quit, it is a cowardly and dishonest way to approach difficulties. This means that a breakdown in communication has occurred. If the congregation is forced to choose sides, no one wins. God has not been consulted. Worship has disintegrated into a power struggle. On the other hand, if the musician is held in respect (i.e., has a working contract), and clergy, musician, and laity meet regularly and approach this discussion prayerfully and lovingly, the results may lead to exciting new directions and possibilities.

I have often heard clergy tout the ministry of the laity. But as soon as there is any conflict, ordained ministry wins. The ministries are not equal. As an ordained clergyperson, I now understand this discourse in a different light. The clergy do feel responsible, ultimately, for decisions that are made. Such decisions may be further complicated because clergy often must answer to the authority of a bishop, synod, board of presbyters, etc. However, if we are seeking worship leaders who feel called to this ministry by God, then shouldn't we be treating both clergy calls and musician calls with equal respect? Shouldn't the question of worship style be treated more carefully in the interview process?

Musicians also need to know themselves. Is your need to control working against the well-being and spiritual growth of the institution? Ego games can be played out very subtly. Silent warfare between musician and clergy undermines the sanctity of the service. An old joke describes this well: A pastor, following a choral anthem, announced the reading from Acts 20:1. Glaring at the choir, he read in a loud voice, "Now when the uproar had ceased...." The choir, silent throughout the sermon, rose immediately following and sang loudly, "Now it is high time to awake out of sleep."

At two regional workshops for the AGO in the summer of 2001, I asked the musicians what the biggest struggle was in their music ministry, what was hindering them from doing the job they felt called to do. The spirited responses included personality conflicts with ministers and staff, concerns for the quality of the worship experience (the issue of excellence versus mediocrity), and dissatisfaction with salaries and benefits. They struggled with the difficulty of feeling God's presence in the midst of all the frenetic activity of the parish and expressed great concern over the future of the profession.

Issues concerning salary and benefits are a constant, especially for part-time sacred musicians who often struggle to piece together full-time jobs, but without any benefits. The salary of a full-time, talented, educated, and hard-working musician who gives a flawless performance of different music each week should be at a high professional level, especially if a congregation has high musical standards and expectations. It should also be noted that because of the tax advantage that clergy people enjoy, the same base salary results in significantly less take-home pay for a musician.

Oftentimes people think, "If the musician is called to be here, why shouldn't they donate their services?" But if the musician is thought of as someone volunteering their services, then they absolutely should get to do anything they want to do. It would be their choice. Perhaps this is where the deepest conflicts arise. The musicians who know that they have been underpaid for years may figure that this donation of time and services allows them to do whatever they want. A poorly paid or underpaid musician will have difficulty being a good team player.

Another current difficulty is the lower number of organists graduating from music schools and conservatories. Most religious institutions want an organist but have little interest in paying an adequate salary even to cover the cost of repaying educational loans, which nowadays can easily top $50,000. What are congregations doing to encourage young people to become sacred musicians? The lack of respect for the gifts and talents required, as evidenced by inadequate salaries and difficult working conditions, does not help stimulate growth in the area of sacred music. Because of the lower number of musicians available, student musicians often take the higher-paying jobs. The lower-paying "student" positions that once offered a kind of apprenticed learning are left vacant. There are ways, however, for a smaller congregation to attract musicians by the care with which they look at the position, benefits, and the possibility of being more flexible with vacation time.

> *A poorly paid or underpaid musician will have difficulty being a good team player.*

Sacred musicians should always ask for a contract. Volunteers who work on personnel and worship committees, vestry, synods, or boards change, as do clergy. Get it in writing. This assures that assumptions that might be made get worked out carefully to the agreement of both parties — before trouble arises. A recent resource that discusses musician salaries, responsibilities, and contracts is *Musicians Called to Serve: A Handbook for the Selection, Employment, and Ministry of Church Musicians*, prepared by the Association of Anglican Musicians.[11] The American Guild of Organists offers a number of professional concerns publications, including its *Professional Concerns Handbook,* which discusses job search, resumes, auditions, contracts, and taxes.[12] Local chapters of the AGO and many denominations have their own publications as well.

It is upsetting to realize that even Johann Sebastian Bach struggled with his church position. After accepting the position of cantor in Leipzig, he wrote: "But since (1) I find that the post is by no means so lucrative as it had been described to me; (2) I have failed to obtain many of the fees pertaining to the office; (3) the place is very expensive; and (4) the authorities are odd and little interested in music, so that I must live amid almost continual vexation, envy, and persecution; accordingly I shall be forced, with God's help, to seek my fortune elsewhere."[13] How sad that such an excellent musician had to grapple with the same issues. But this is also further proof that the issues are systemic. Bach did not end up leaving Leipzig, but continued in that position for another twenty years until his death.

We know what a dysfunctional relationship looks like between clergy and musician. But what would define a healthy relationship? How might it operate?

The Reverend John E. Kitigawa, rector of St. Philip's in the Hills Episcopal Church in Tucson, tells wonderful stories about his time as curate at Calvary Church (Episcopal) in New York City toward the end of Calvin Hampton's tenure there as church musician.[14] Kitigawa speaks of informal meetings on Monday in which they would look at the readings, and Kitigawa, if he were preaching that Sunday, would begin to figure out in what direction the sermon might go. They would go to the sanctuary, where Hampton would play through hymns, and they would decide together which would work best for the liturgy. Then Hampton would talk about the anthem. Sometimes he would pull something out, and they would both agree that it was perfect. Other times he would admit that he did not have anything. Kitigawa would say, "Well, what are you going to do?" And Hampton would reply, "I'll just have to write a new one." And he would, by Thursday night.

I always laugh when I hear Kitigawa tell those stories about such an amazing and gifted composer and church musician. I wonder if that is the way it is in heaven — composers churning out new anthems for heavenly choirs as brilliantly new and creative ideas keeping popping forth on how to praise God.

But on earth, this does not always work. Most choirs need to rehearse weeks in advance to allow the singers, often amateurs, sufficient time to learn the music. Even choirs with professional singers would have difficulty learning a brand-new anthem from a composer's manuscript in three days. And many musicians at religious institutions are not composers (although there are a surprising number who manage to come up with something when they have to!). Whether or not this kind of relationship is practical, let's talk about what is wonderful about it.

The greatest gift about this particular relationship is that there is respect on both sides. Both musician and minister recognize that the other has something to offer and that God will work through them if they work together. An idea will come. They will be inspired. They can count on it.

This relationship represents the coming together of different personalities and ways of knowing. True worship happens precisely in this tension, in the holy space that is created between the verbal and non-verbal. The mystery is revealed. Not just through words. Not just through music. But through both together, "The Word made flesh..."

Not all clergy are amenable to working with the musician on hymn selection, and vice versa. The constraints of busy schedules are always a problem. But if this cannot be done as a corporate endeavor every week, maybe it could at least be given an opportunity once a month. Struggling over hymn selection can actually be a joyful and playful experience. When the Spirit is given the opportunity to work ahead of time between worship leaders, the congregation will know it. The worship is far more likely to be inspired.

A defining question is whether or not clergy, musicians and staff actually *experience* worship together outside of the worship service. If that never happens, no wonder the worship service does not feel particularly holy. Collegial relationships that include genuine prayer and in which pastoral concerns are shared in an environment of trust and respect should be the goal of every religious institution. *The best way to improve worship is to improve the relationships between the worship leaders.*

One of Calvin Hampton's most popular hymn tunes, *St. Helena,* is set to the text "There's a wideness in God's mercy" by Frederick William Faber. The second verse begins "There is no place where earth's sorrows are more felt than up in heaven; there is no place where earth's failings have such kindly judgment given."[15] Sometimes it seems as if the greatest gulf to bridge can be between stubborn ministers and obstinate musicians. I imagine that the angels, the composer-saints, musician-saints, and clergy-saints must cry more over those broken relationships and lost opportunities to lead the people of God in praise than anything else. With the help of God and with prayer, that place of brokenness can become a place for God's tremendous mercy.

Nine

OUR HUMANITY

I N 1938, Nadia Boulanger, composer, conductor, organist, and teacher of some of the greatest musical minds of the twentieth century, conducted the Boston Symphony Orchestra in a performance of the Fauré *Requiem*. When asked what it felt like to be the first female conductor of the Boston Symphony Orchestra, she replied, "I've been a woman for a little over fifty years and have gotten over my initial astonishment."[1]

Despite her lack of interest in contributing to the male-female dialectic, she nonetheless had to struggle with the uninterested and disruptive behavior of the all-male orchestra. Halting the first rehearsal, she admonished them not to underestimate the beauty and depth of feeling behind the *Requiem* despite its apparent simplicity. She won them over. After an inspired performance, Serge Koussevitzky and every member of the orchestra lined up to greet her on stage in full view of the audience.[2]

I would like to say, like Nadia Boulanger, that I have gotten over my initial astonishment at being a woman. But I certainly have not gotten over my astonishment at the behavior that I have witnessed because of my gender — the sexism and sexual harassment that I have endured in both academic and ecclesiastic settings. The story of Adam and Eve, which has traditionally blamed Eve for all of the evil in the world, has been particularly problematic for me because it perpetuates misogyny. But in more recent years, I have begun to realize what a gift this story is. Rather than admitting their failure to treasure their relationship with God as more important than any other relationship, *both* man and woman fixed blame outside of themselves. They both blamed "other." In so doing, they destroyed their corporate identity and mutual trust. Without the solace of this community of two — this embryonic congregation, so to speak — they became afraid to stand alone before God. They felt shame. They forgot that they had been created *together* in the image of God. "And God created man in His image, in the image of God He created him; male and female He created them" (Gen. 1:27).[3]

I am still mourning the death of a former student. He started taking organ lessons with me when he was in prep school, over twenty years ago. As a student, he was not the most distinguished, but he fell in love with playing the organ. And I witnessed it.

I watched him discover the profound joy and peace of practicing in an empty church — of seeing the light shift through stained-glass windows as the day wore on, and of breaking the darkness with light-filled notes. His joy was infectious as his feet began to master exercises and scales and as the coordination of hands and body improved. He marveled at the different sonorities, and thrilled at the sheer power of full organ. He discovered Bach. I loved teaching him.

A few years ago in January, the family began to plan a memorial concert for May. That was when I heard the news that it was suicide. And it was only at the concert that I heard from his beloved partner of six years that he had hanged himself.

On a recent Mark Steiner radio show in Baltimore, gay men and women were advising young people as to the appropriate time to "come out." They all said that you have to have tremendous support and good friends, but that you can never anticipate how people will respond. You might want to wait until you get older and have a thicker skin. And then someone said, "And, of course, you have to be in therapy!"

Why do you have to be in therapy if you want to be truthful about being a homosexual in our society? Have we branded ourselves so profoundly with our heterosexism that we cannot even tolerate *knowing* if someone is different than we are — or than we *think* we are? How can that blindness be representative of the love of God?

The Reverend Peter Gomes, Plummer Professor of Christian Morals at Harvard College and my former homiletics professor, did not "come out" publicly until he had been teaching at Harvard for almost twenty years. Even then, he did not expect to reveal his identity at a rally demonstrating against hatred of homosexuals on the campus. Writing about the incident in *The Good Book,* he said, "I gave my speech, and naïvely thought that my disclosure of my own homosexuality would serve to substantiate the Christian message of reconciliation in diversity and equality in Christ. I, however, rather than my message, became the subject of attention."[4]

I asked Gomes a few years later how he felt about this truth telling and whether it had changed things. He said that the positive response had been overwhelming. Of course, there was negative response, but less than he expected. He wished he had done it sooner. Despite the difficulties, he writes, "I nevertheless found this experience to be one of the most formative and rewarding of my ministry."[5]

As a woman, I have struggled with sexism and sexual harassment. Over the years I have begun to understand how these forms of misogyny operate, and how to avoid participating in societal games. In the midst of my anger and pain, I have discovered that God loves me for who I am, and that She rejoices that I am female.

No, by saying that God has a female side, I am not denying that God is also male. I just have come to believe that the Holy One who has created this awesome, magnificent, expanding universe is much bigger than a white, heterosexual, middle-aged man.

But here's the thing: when you look at me, you know that I am female. If you are black, Hispanic, physically handicapped, people know just by looking at you. If you are gay in our culture, you always have the option of passing as heterosexual. It does not mean that you do not long to be able to be honest about who you are. But you are rewarded for your secrecy. Your behavior, somehow, is considered more proper. And it seems as if everyone plays along with this game until someone cannot pull it off any more and he or she commits suicide.

Something has to change. We cannot go on pretending that any of these identity games are healthy, truthful, or even that they work. The recent movie *Brokeback Mountain* is a beautifully told story of two men who fall in love with each other, but are forced to lead double lives at a time when homosexuality was not tolerated in America. The tragedy is not just the waste of their own happiness, but also the extent of the shattered relationships that are left in their wake. Lies beget more lies. Pretending to be something that we are not is dangerous to others as well as to our own souls. Game playing strangles our belief systems.

So then how can we create an environment that is not only safe for people who are like us, but also safe for people who are not? We cannot just pass down the morality of our elders. The world has changed. Our morality needs to grow and mature. Stereotypes

102

are based on fear and prejudice. Unless our family systems were very unusual fifty years ago, contact with people who were different was probably not encouraged. Expanding our understanding of family to include our neighbor enables us to view all of humanity as brother and sister. Can't we pray ourselves into some new place, a new vision of worship in which all are invited and welcomed — in which all kinds of relationships are blessed simply because we all need God's blessing in getting relationships right? Isn't it time for a New Church, a New Temple to rise up out of the ashes of the old?

> *Pretending to be something that we are not is dangerous to others as well as to our own souls.*

Eve is an archetype symbolizing more that just woman. Because she represents "other," she can also represent every difference that God has created, and every difference with which a society may be uncomfortable: from gender, race, and religion to level of education, income, musical preference, and lifestyle. The serpent continues to trick us again and again, trying to separate us from God by separating us from each other. Our true joy, however, can be found only in singing praise to our Maker together. Somehow we must seek to be reunited

on holy ground. By working to break down our prejudices, to change our language so that it corresponds
to our evolving understanding of the Divine, and to expand our compassion for those who are different, we will
begin to appreciate the hugeness and sheer majesty of
creation. No, we are not all the same. But together, that
is *all* of us, we are created in the image of God.

Ten

WORKING OUTSIDE
YOUR FAITH TRADITION

I SAW A BUMPER STICKER the other day that read, "Militant Agnostic. I don't know and you don't know either!" *The New Shorter Oxford English Dictionary* gives two definitions of an agnostic: "A person who holds the view that nothing can be known of the existence of God or of anything beyond material phenomena," and also "a person who is uncertain or noncommittal about a particular thing." I learned something. I had never thought of agnostics as running the gamut from fanatic to casual just as in other religions. Why should there *not* be evangelical agnostics?

We musicians in religious institutions often are not a member of the denomination or religion we serve. A Methodist may be working in a Roman Catholic church, an Episcopalian in a Jewish synagogue, and a Baptist in a Unitarian church. Leading the musical portion of another congregation's worship with integrity provides an unusual opportunity to experience a different corporate spirituality. The tolerance that is necessary changes us and changes our understanding of God. Our world gets bigger.

Fanaticism does not allow for tolerance. Fanatics in any culture or religion (including agnosticism) see their way as the only way. If we care about living in a peaceful society with different kinds of people, then it is important to respect each other's belief systems and support the free will of all persons to have their own life's philosophy. Is it possible to be tolerant of others and still be true to our own integrity and beliefs?

The tolerance that is necessary changes us and changes our understanding of God.

Abraham Heschel (1907–70), rabbi, scholar, professor, and activist, was unusual in his ability to articulate the bigger picture. In a 1966 lecture "No Religion Is an Island" given at Union Theological Seminary, Heschel stated:

We are all involved with one another. Spiritual betrayal on the part of one of us affects the faith of all of us. Views adopted in one community have an impact on other communities. Today, religious isolationism is a myth. For all the profound differences in perspective and substance, Judaism is sooner or later affected by the intellectual, moral, and spiritual events within the Christian society, and vice versa.[1]

Heschel worries about the cynicism and nihilism that plague the world. He calls for people of different faith commitments to pray for each other. Viewing every person as representing all humanity, he says, "Many things on earth are precious, some are holy, humanity is holy of holies."[2] Meeting a human being, therefore, provides "an opportunity to sense the image of God, the *presence* of God."[3] He continues:

> I suggest that the most significant basis for meeting of men of different religious traditions is the level of fear and trembling, of humility and contrition, where our individual moments of faith are mere waves in the endless ocean of mankind's reaching out for God, ... where our souls are swept away by the awareness of the urgency of answering God's commandment, while stripped of pretension and conceit we sense the tragic insufficiency of human faith.[4]

Heschel, a Jew who escaped from Warsaw barely six weeks before the Nazi "disaster,"[5] calls for a level of tolerance that continues to resonate profoundly in the twenty-first century. Indeed, if the world neglects to heed a voice such as his, the continuing struggles between competing fanaticisms and ideologies can only lead to global disaster. The solution is to hold our faith with humility, making certain that our belief is in God, not in the sanctity of our dogma.

How can you prepare yourself, therefore, if you are beginning a position in a church or synagogue that is outside of your religious experience?

1. Treat the situation as an opportunity for learning new things.

2. Ask for help.

3. Have respect for what you do not understand. Don't make presumptions.

4. Be open to what is different.

5. Go to the library and find a good historical overview of this religion or denomination. How does its history influence the style of worship?

6. Take home the hymnal or worship book. Read it carefully, especially prefaces, which might tell you about what is important.

7. Look at the prayers. What do you notice?

8. What is the congregation's view of silence? Do they have a more introverted or extraverted spirituality? Are you comfortable with their spirituality?

9. What is of utmost importance during the service?

10. How does the congregation define good worship or a good worship experience? How can you help that happen?

Most ministers will rejoice in frank conversations about what is new to you and will answer any questions you might have. This is a great opportunity for you to hold up what is distinctive about this congregation and to question worship practices that may have arisen from bad habits.

The musician who is truly tolerant is unusual and is to be commended in this angry world. In his essay "What Ecumenism Is," Heschel writes, "Different are the languages of prayer, but the tears are the same."[6]

Genuine tolerance for other beliefs is one of the ways in which the world can be healed, the breach narrowed between mind-sets and worldviews. When you work outside your faith tradition, you become an ambassador for your belief system, so represent it well. The surprise is to discover what hymns, words, and tunes have migrated from one religious institution to another. Once acclimated to the needs of the congregation, a sensitive musician might be able to share music from past experience and repertoire that complements the congregation's spirituality and adds to its musical corpus. I remain amazed that "A Mighty Fortress Is Our God," the anthem of the Protestant Reformation, has found its way into the Catholic hymnal.[7] We are united at the deepest place when we sing the same song.

Finally, don't feel bad if you decide that playing for a different denomination or religion is not for you. Not all musicians feel comfortable playing in churches or synagogues that are not their own. Your spiritual journey may also change course, and what used to feel good and right may have become a strain. Only you can be the judge of this. The question to ask yourself is, "Where can I lead worship most joyfully?"

May you work with integrity and respect for those around you. And no matter where you find yourself, may your music making be filled with love and compassion.

Eleven

PREDICTABLE
SEASONAL TENSION

YEARS AGO one Christmas Eve, after a particularly elaborate two-hour service in which I had conducted two choirs and a brass quintet and played the organ, a parishioner asked me why all the music was so sad. "It wasn't sad," I insisted, surprised by the comment, hurt, exhausted, and incapable of discussing the matter rationally. But later as I thought it over, I realized that most of the music had been sad. On the personal side, my father-in-law had been diagnosed with a brain tumor and had only a few months to live. Besides this, however, I began to realize that I had always tended to hear Christmas as bittersweet, in a minor key, doleful and yet exquisitely sung. Those were my favorite carols and anthems. A fast, sprightly carol could work well on Christmas Day, but seemed quite difficult to accomplish on Christmas Eve.

Didn't I feel joy that God had become incarnate in Christ Jesus? Yes, but Good Friday was still to come. Okay, but if I knew that much of the story, why stop there? What about the Resurrection? I began to ask myself what theology was actually influencing my choice of music, articulation, dynamic level, and tempi. Was it expediency? laziness? or did my half-baked theology, whether intentional or not, have more power over my decisions than I was aware? Where was my joy? Was I able to give my music making back to God as a gift, or was I holding the congregation hostage to my own anger and bitterness at where I was in life?

Knowing yourself and what times of year are particularly difficult for you are critical insights for professionalism and excellence. When do family pressures most encroach on your practice time? When do extra-musical activities hamper good musical preparation and presence? How can you learn from your less than perfect offerings so that they do not become a regular feature?

Sometimes a religious institution expects that an organist will always be able to play and conduct the choir at the same time. This may be possible during a fairly uncomplicated service, but may be too much for you during a complex liturgy. Knowing that you need to hire someone to help you is the first step toward musical sanity. Be insistent. A retired choral director may be honored to be asked to conduct, and may also bring added enthusiasm that reenergizes you.

If someone particularly close to you or to choir members has died during a major liturgical festival, be mindful of that as you program music for the next year, knowing that you or the choir will probably be emotionally fragile. Do you remember to assess how well the music worked following these festival occasions? Have you ever recorded the service and listened to it later? What was the real problem on Christmas Eve this year? Was it really that there was not enough time between services, or were your expectations for what your volunteer choir could muster too high? Don't forget that Christmas time and the High Holy Days are especially difficult times for everyone. This is a time of extra family tension, societal depression, and higher addictive tendencies. How can you factor that into your music program?

Church of the Holy Nativity, where I was vicar for ten years, is an Episcopal urban mission church. Housed in a former automotive parts store, it is located in an African American neighborhood of northwest Baltimore called Park Heights, which struggles with abandoned buildings and persistent drug problems. The congregation is three-quarters black, one-quarter white, and encompasses people from all over the city with a variety of class, cultural, educational, and professional backgrounds. One of the members faithfully brings mentally challenged people from her place of employment to church every Sunday. This is a diverse and wondrous body, connected weekly by Eucharist in a circle around the altar.

Despite the differences, or perhaps because of them, there is a spirit present that feels light-filled and joyous. Holy Nativity lives in a liminal place — one of those "thin" places that seems to be closer to heaven than earth. Those who have the courage to step across the threshold are welcomed with open arms.

You do not have to be perfect, just faithful.

While I was there, we struggled with many issues: children at-risk in homes or schools that have not been supportive of their special needs; major structural repairs to an old building; trying to provide a safe place for the neighborhood children to get tutoring help and a free summer program to keep them active and learning; pastoral situations surrounding addictions and violence; and the vast assortment of personal and spiritual needs that all people seem to share in common.

But the hardest time on the streets of Park Heights is the late fall, when darkness descends earlier and earlier. The children are more fearful of walking home from the after-school program; flickering shadows intensify the feeling that evil is winning. Stories of violence and crime, two ever-present struggles in Baltimore, take on mythic proportions. Advent feels critical, and by

Christmas all are desperate to be saved by a compassionate God who reaches down to touch us in our humanity.

On an Advent retreat at St. Margaret's House in Philadelphia, as I struggled in my prayer life with some of the more difficult aspects of ministry at Holy Nativity, I kept seeing the glowing and beautiful faces of our children. I had begun a choir as a way to teach these children theology. The spiritual warfare with which they contend is real. Songs with clear theological intention had become the most beloved and helpful. I found that having them memorize the words gave them something to hold on to when they found themselves in dangerous situations.

Finding solace for myself in one of the litanies on the name of Jesus, I was inspired to incorporate it into a Christmas text that my husband quickly set to music when I returned home. The children had no trouble remembering the words, which seemed to belong to them.

The children grew older, and the choir disbanded. But the song remained a staple of our Christmas Eve service. Two years ago on Christmas Eve, one of our troubled sixteen-year-olds who was flirting with inner-city street life chose to sing this hymn as a solo. She sang it beautifully and from the bottom of her heart. I was moved to tears.

O Holy Nativity

1 O ho - ly na - ti - vi - ty, birth of our King, O Je - sus, most gen - tle, your
2 O ho - ly na - ti - vi - ty, star of great light, O Je - sus, most hum - ble, O
3 O ho - ly na - ti - vi - ty, sent from a - bove, O Je - sus, most per - fect, O

prai - ses we sing.___ Our wait is now o - ver. You came as a child. The
Je - sus most bright,___ we thought you for - got us, but now you ap - pear. You
Je - sus, our Love,___ please hold us for - e - ver. O come let us bring our

dark - ness means no - thing, O Je - - - - sus, most mild.___
make us so hap - py, O Je - - - - sus, most dear.___
prayers and our prai - ses to Je - - - - sus, our King.___

Words: Victoria R. Sirota (b. 1949)
Music: Holy Nativity, Robert Sirota (b. 1949)

That spring was one of the hardest periods for our little congregation as we had to welcome with open arms the children of our children. Quite a number of unwed teenagers became pregnant and gave birth. It seemed like an epidemic. And yet, providing two of these little boys with godparents at the Easter Vigil, claiming them as part of our family and part of the fabric of our being, felt profoundly significant. Perhaps "O Holy Nativity" will become their song as well, speaking to them of a love that is beyond what is humanly possible.

At a worship workshop in Richmond, Virginia, a few years ago,[1] a group of religious musicians sat and talked about the ways in which we could be more pastoral to ourselves and to our choirs at times of seasonal stress. Simply thinking about the issue a month and a half before Christmas was a great help. We could still remember the difficulties but were able to think of them separately from our own tension and exhaustion. Choosing simpler anthems, anthems that were more familiar, easier service music, less music for the choir and more hymns for the congregation, letting the brass quintet play the prelude and postlude instead of the organist were possible suggestions.

Most important in stressful times, however, is for sacred musicians — organists, pianists, conductors, soloists, and choir — to remember to pray together. Don't say you don't have the time. If you don't have the time, then you need the prayer all the more. A short prayer

117

will suffice. Remembering to offer your corporate gifts to the Almighty puts you all in a better place. Excellence is the goal during rehearsals, but during the service the goal is worship. The greatest last-minute gift that you can give yourself is to remember that you do not have to be perfect, just faithful. And, by all means, ask for heavenly help.

Twelve

DEATH AND DYING

WHAT DO YOU SAY to those who are dying? How do you let them feel your presence gently and honor them by keeping watch with them for more than just the few seconds it takes to mumble greetings and a quick prayer? What can you give them to help send them on their way? How can you help release them from this life and from the shame of dying, of abandoning us, and help them move on into the light?

As I wrote these words a number of years ago, Violet, the mother of four and grandmother of eight, lay hovering between life and death in the hospice ward of a Baltimore hospital. I went to visit her, but after having said the words of the Twenty-third Psalm and the Lord's Prayer, found that I did not want to leave her side. Despite the fact that she was semi-conscious, she seemed to be present.

Rather than standing there in awkward silence, I began to sing to her. First, I sang songs from my own cultural heritage, familiar hymns from my past, but she did not respond. Then I began to search my memory for African American spirituals or Gospel songs that might

119

have meaning for her. Unable to remember most of the words, at least I was confident of the melodies I was humming. The one that elicited the strongest response was Thomas A. Dorsey's "Precious Lord." She seemed agitated, as if she wanted me to get the words. She was trying to tell me something.

It was a few days before I could return. What could I bring her? She had no need of anything physical. She was dying. Then I remembered her response to "Precious Lord." I stopped what I was doing, grabbed a hymnal, and wrote out the text to that hymn and three others in my pocket calendar. What I could give her were the words to the songs that she loved.

I stood beside her bed, prayed over her, and said the words of the psalm. She seemed to be joining me although no words escaped from her lips and her eyes were tightly closed. I opened my pocket calendar, found the page with the hymn texts, and timidly started singing "Precious Lord." Her body kept absolutely still. She listened with every fiber of her being.

When I got to the second verse, a miracle happened. It was as if I heard the words for the first time, even though we sang them often at Church of the Holy Nativity. "When my way grows drear, precious Lord, linger near, When my life is almost gone." She became agitated, her foot moving wildly and her body swaying with the music. Then from some deep place, Violet began to moan. Her voice, like the unearthly sound of a whale, accompanied me wordlessly as I sang "Hear my cry, hear my call, Hold my hand, lest I fall, Take my hand, precious Lord, Lead me on."[1] That is what she was trying to tell me. She wanted to share with me how she felt. She was telling me that she was prepared to die because these words were etched in her soul, and they had now become her comfort. This was her prayer. When I left Violet, I was totally shaken, awed, and exhilarated.

Why "Precious Lord"? Because somehow in the depths of Thomas Dorsey's grief over the unexpected death of his wife in childbirth (the baby died soon after), he allowed himself to infuse the words with genuine suffering and yearning for God's presence in the midst of the sometimes horrible agony and incomprehensible mystery of life on earth.[2] In Dorsey's words, the song "came twisting out of my very heart."[3] His pain became Violet's as she prepared to give up her loved ones. I am grateful that I could give them to each other at that awesome moment in the presence of the Holy One.

Death always seems to surprise us. What is the best way to deal with the death of a loved one? How can we make sense of our fragile mortality?

One way is through ritual. People need to gather together and process the loss. Attention must be paid. The world must stop, if only for an hour or two, and mourn communally. Some sense must be made of it all. We seek cosmic answers and divine comfort.

Another way to make sense of death is to allow our lives to change. The most amazing and beautiful miracles often occur surrounding the most outrageous tragedies. In counseling sessions, I am continually awed at how death can be the catalyst for great personal growth and change. Not that people are ever glad someone has died, but they have taken the loss and woven it into their lives by allowing a real transformation to occur. Somehow that transformation becomes a tribute to the memory of the one who died.

Do not underestimate the importance of your pastoral ministry.

In my own life, if it were not for the death of a number of dear friends and loved ones over a relatively short period of time, I do not think that I would have had the courage to change professions and become a priest. Somehow I needed that prodding in order to think in new ways, to envision something different.

The death of someone close pulls the rug out from under us. Every experience of it is a unique surprise. Each time we relearn for ourselves that life is fragile. We are reminded that we do not have unlimited time with each other.

Like Thomas Dorsey, we can also allow the experience to inspire new compositions, new creative work, a new hymn. Some of the greatest pieces ever written were inspired by the death of a loved one. Or we may wish to change the way we play a piece or conduct an anthem — greater space, less fear of silence, a more profound phrasing. We transcend death when we use it as the motivation to create new life.

And finally, we can begin to take the gift of our own life more seriously. In *Traits of a Healthy Spirituality*, Melanie Svoboda quotes the story of a rabbi who prayed to God, " 'O Lord, make me holy! Make me like Moses!' But God replied to him, 'What need have I of another Moses? I already have one! But what I really could use is you!' "[4] What is your assignment while you are here? How can God use you? How can you use your gifts and talents to bring people together and to share God's great gift of love?

I have been to so many different kinds of funerals. Violet's took three hours and had all the drama of powerful African American worship. The organist was eventually joined by a drummer and guitarist as the congregation was encouraged to cry and mourn, to stomp on Satan, and finally to dance out the door in anticipation of the Resurrection.

Another particularly poignant funeral was that of the fifteen-year-old child of a Peabody faculty member a few years ago. In support of his colleague, organ professor Donald Sutherland played his heart out. The chorus of Peabody students was breathtaking. Everyone present was grateful for the tremendous generosity of the musical offering. It made a difference.

Do not underestimate the importance of your pastoral ministry as a musician at a time of mourning. At those moments of great sorrow, we lean on your faith. You walk us through the pain and bring us to the joy of hope that our faith promises. The love that you pour into a phrase is palpable. The gentleness with which you guide us through our tears is a gift of grace. And when you turn the corner in the service, and carry us up to heaven in angelic arms, we are transported beyond the veil. For those brief moments we can feel God's love and we know for certain that we are being held in God's embrace.

Thirteen

SHOULD YOU QUIT?

CALLS ARE ALWAYS time sensitive. No one else can tell you when you should leave a position. But sometimes you begin to have a nagging feeling that the time is coming, especially if personnel have changed and the institution seems to be moving in a different direction.

Let's say that you are classically trained and that you are being told to change the style of music at one of the two services of which you are in charge. How do you decide whether to stay or leave?

1. Assess the situation. Is this the same position that I felt called to when I came? What is different?

2. Do I trust the clergy? Can I have professional and honest conversation about changes in liturgy and worship style?

3. Do these changes in style make sense theologically? To what ministries does God seem to be calling this congregation?

4. What are my greatest gifts and talents? Are they being used? Does the music ministry complement the other active ministries or seem disconnected?

125

5. Being totally honest with myself, am I *interested* in learning a new musical style? Is the congregation open to "blended" services, or do they wish to change over completely to a new style?

6. Does the music ministry have the budget to hire extra musicians to play this new music, or to allow me to take a course or study with someone in order to broaden my skills?

7. Do I feel respected by those in authority, or am I being shamed or made to feel inadequate despite my education, training, background, and experience?

8. What would I lose by leaving this position? Would I grieve inconsolably? Do I feel called to new areas of growth in this place?

9. What would I gain by leaving this position? Would it feel like a great weight had been lifted from my shoulders? Does the idea of a new position fill me with a sense of joy?

10. Would it be possible for me to move to a different location at this time? What would be the advantages and disadvantages?

Figuring out what makes you the happiest is a very important step toward self-awareness. For example, if you are a builder of music programs, your current program is successful, and you are surprisingly bored, you may be feeling the urge to help another congregation with good potential get their music program going. This may be the best use of your gifts as well as the place where you will find your greatest joy.

> *Figuring out what makes you the happiest is a very important step toward self-awareness.*

Changing positions is stressful and involves a grieving process. You are changing the people that you see on a regular basis. Process this carefully with people you trust. It is this very aspect of risk-taking, however, that can also make you feel younger and reenergize you. If your gifts and skills are stagnating where you are, this may be the way to reintroduce delight into your life. Remember, there is a shortage of good sacred musicians. You may not be able to find a job in the exact location you want or at the exact salary you want, but you will be able to find something. You can always go on the American Guild of Organists substitute list while you are looking.[1] Doing supply work may help you discern what you are looking for more objectively.

If you are leaving a position, don't forget: You are firing them. Be gentle. You hold the power. How would you like to be treated if you were being fired? Be as kind as possible. You may need a reference at a later date.

And do not be surprised if they end up having to offer your position to someone else at a higher salary. This, actually, is the best way to raise salaries in your area!

An important indicator of spiritual state is one's prayer life. If you have trouble praying, are stuck in a place of whining and self-pity, and are angry with God, this may also be an indication that you need to do something differently or move on.

Pray about where exactly God may be calling you, and talk to colleagues whom you trust. Whether you stay or whether you leave, do you have the faith and courage to take the risk of making changes, to step out and trust God with your future? May God hold you gently through this process of discernment.

Fourteen

FINAL THOUGHTS

A T THE END of the book of 1 Kings, we find the great prophet Elijah close to burnout. He tells the Lord that he is ready to die. But God calls him to Mount Horeb, where he experiences a theophany, a vision of God. Surprisingly, the Lord is not in the wind, earthquake, or fire but in a sound of "sheer silence" (1 Kings 19:11–12). One of Elijah's new directives is to find Elisha and anoint him to be his prophetic successor. The Lord has heard Elijah's cry.

As Elijah is about to be taken up by God, he asks Elisha for his last request of him. Elisha asks for a "double portion" of Elijah's spirit (2 Kings 2:9). I have always found this passage troubling. How arrogant and presumptuous of this apprentice prophet. How can he hope to be a greater prophet than Elijah? Elijah notes that it is a difficult thing, but then says if Elisha can see him being taken away — if he is given the eyes of a visionary — then his wish has been granted. Elisha cries out, "Father, father!" as he watches his mentor being taken up to heaven in a whirlwind (2 Kings 2:11–12).

From the standpoint of the sacred musician, this passage makes perfect sense. Of course we have the audacity to ask for more inspiration than that of our teachers. And a really great teacher will rejoice that the flame is being carried on with equal if not more passion and conviction. Elijah probably thought, "Now, finally, I can depart in peace. The prophetic voice of the Almighty is in good hands."

I remember knocking on the studio door of Professor Garth Peacock, my organ teacher at Oberlin Conservatory of Music, the day before my senior recital. "I can't do it," I said. "I can't play a memorized recital tomorrow." He said, "Yes, you can. I've heard you do it three times already." One of the most important gifts my teacher gave me was his confidence when my own had vanished.

We stand on the shoulders of those who go before us. We strive to do our part to carry the flame. Lessons that we have learned from great mentors and teachers, memories of the sheer beauty and inspiration of great performances that we have heard, and the passion and love of music that have been instilled in us by others are added to our own gifts, our own love of music. This, then, is the flame we carry throughout our lives. What we tend to forget is how much of this flame was a gift from others, and how much of it was a gift from God. And sometimes we also forget that we will need to let go of it, to pass it on. We need to nurture the young talent of others, to pass on the secrets that we have learned. We need to make sure that the great music, inspired hymn playing, wondrous choral singing, and beautiful chanting that preceded us will continue long after we are gone.

This legacy is profound. We carry the tradition. We must never forget the majesty and grandeur of the role we have been given.

Paul Hume, musician and music critic for the *Washington Post* from 1947 to 1982, addressed the American Guild of Organists Convention in 1982: "Do you realize what you can do with your music? . . . May I suggest, strongly I hope, that in churches where music is chosen imaginatively, and performed with taste and style and beauty, that it is often the music that captures the hearts of many in the congregation." He goes on to say, "One person is all it takes to make the difference. One person who knows the music that can transform a congregation from a passive or indifferent group of listeners into an active, absorbed audience who, through great music, beautifully performed, may find a new approach to God."[1]

You are far more important than you think. Do not despair. Do not allow bullying voices to take over the holy space. Stand up for what is good and right and true.

Work toward better working conditions, higher salaries and benefits. If you have trouble doing this for yourself, then do it for the good of the profession. In order for our profession to grow at this time of fewer organ students, church and synagogue musicians must be able to make more than a living wage. Keep bringing information about salary tables, contracts, and benefits packages to your employer. Treat your own position and the position of other musicians with whom you work with respect. If you leave, leave the position in a better place than when you arrived.

> *Treat your clergy as you would like to be treated.*

Be kind to yourself and take good care of yourself. You cannot do your best work if you are not getting enough sleep, not practicing enough, and not preparing scores well enough in advance. If workaholism is a consistent pattern with you, take it up with a professional. Why try to fill up every second of every day? What are you running away from — silence? When do you allow yourself simply to receive God's bountiful love and bask in it?

Do not allow perfectionism to take over the sanctuary. This is a form of idolatry that can only lead to anger, self-pity, or self-righteousness. Try at all times to do your best, but be kind to those with whom you work. Give them the benefit of the doubt. Trust them and love them. You are called to this position not to be perfect but to be faithful. That means admitting your mistakes, learning from them and moving on. If you are working for a perfectionist who has lost awareness of the presence of the Divine and the sheer joy of worship, determine whether such an environment is one in which to do your best work.

It does not matter what kind of instrument you are playing or how big it is. Get the most music out of it that you can. It does not matter how large your choir is or how well balanced it is. Make music as joyously as possible. Enjoy the room, the space, the people, and the gifts of the congregation. Treat your position as a calling, and you will find greater clarity about how to treat difficult situations.

Treat your clergy as you would like to be treated. Be the model of a faithful steward, trustworthy friend, and pastoral presence. Be kind but honest. Say the same things to their face that you would say behind their back. Build up trust and loyalty. If this is not possible, then consider how lethal this situation may become to your good health and your spiritual well-being. Life is too short. Move on.

Stay in touch with musical colleagues. Keep attending conferences and conventions. Learn new repertoire and get new ideas. Be inspired by the gifts and talents of others. If you are jealous of someone else, pay attention and use this self-knowledge to strive for what that person has that you are lacking. Find healthy ways to have fun.

Try to live a life that is holy. If deception is part of your daily routine, you may find that this wears down your self-esteem over time. Live in the light. Use your gifts and talents in praise of the Almighty and for the glory of God.

And finally, don't forget to pray. Nancy Roth writes, "Prayer is the means whereby we let the Spirit of God breathe in and through us."[2] When we allow ourselves to be open to God, then we can begin to offer our music to God as prayer. Breathing in and out, relaxed and open, no longer ruled by our own neediness and passions, we can begin to explore fully our relationship with God, a relationship that will inevitably transform all of our relationships with the people of God. This exploration is what others are craving to hear in our music. The role of sacred musician, like the role of the minister, is that of spiritual guide. We cannot perform our duties adequately unless we take our own spiritual journey seriously, offering our music to God with no strings attached as a form of prayer.

Rededicate yourself to this noble profession and carry your flame with joy. May angels guard and protect you. And may you, like Elijah, experience God's presence for yourself and pass the Spirit on to another. Go in peace.

NOTES

Introduction

Sections of this introduction were first published as "From the Chaplain," *The American Organist* (August 2001): 33.

1. Claiming the Call of Sacred Musician

This chapter first appeared as "The Call of the Sacred Musician" in "From the Chaplain," *The American Organist* (October 2001): 12.

    1. See Matthew 4:1–11; Mark 1:12–13; Luke 4:1–13.

    2. C. S. Lewis, "Screwtape Proposes a Toast," *The Screwtape Letters* (New York: Touchstone, 1996), 128. "Screwtape Proposes a Toast" first published in C. S. Lewis, *The World's Last Night* (New York: Harcourt Brace Jovanovich, 1959).

2. Music as Theology

Sections of this chapter appeared as "An Exploration of Music as Theology," *ARTS* 5, no. 3 (1993): 24–28; reprinted in *Theological Education* 31, no. 1 (1994): 165–73; and *ARTS* 11, no. 2 (1999): 18–23.

    1. Johann Sebastian Bach, "Prelude" from *The Unaccompanied Cello Suite, No. 1 in G major*, BWV 1007, as performed by YoYo Ma.

    2. Sponsored by the Yale Institute of Sacred Music, Worship and the Arts, this Consultation on Music as Theology took place at Auburn Theological Seminary in New York City on April 25, 1992.

3. This is the familiar first line of the song. The title of this selection is "Somewhere."

4. Paul Henry Lang, "The Patrimonium Musicae Sacrae and the Task of Sacred Music Today," *Sacred Music and Liturgy Reform after Vatican II,* Proceedings of the Fifth International Church Music Congress, Chicago-Milwaukee, August 21–28, 1966, ed. Johannes Overath (Rome: Consociatio Internationalis Musicae Sacrae, 1969), 248.

5. "O Little Town of Bethlehem," hymns 78 and 79, The Hymnal 1982 (New York: Church Publishing, 1985).

6. E. E. Ryden, *The Story of Christian Hymnody* (Philadelphia: Fortress Press, 1959), 549.

7. Ibid., 549–50.

8. Nancy Roth, *The Breath of God: An Approach to Prayer* (Cambridge, Mass.: Cowley Publications, 1990), 9.

9. Abraham of Nathpar, "On Prayer: How It Is Necessary for Someone Who Prays to Be Eager and Vigilant in Himself," in *The Syriac Fathers on Prayer and the Spiritual Life,* introduction and trans. Sebastian Brock (Kalamazoo, Mich.: Cistercian Publications, 1987), 192–93.

10. Edward Farley, as stated at the Consultation on Music as Theology, Auburn Theological Seminary, April 25, 1992. His reference to "Thou" is from Martin Buber, *I and Thou,* 2nd ed., trans. Ronald Gregor Smith (New York: First Scribner Classic/Collier Edition, 1987).

3. The Spirituality of the Sacred Musician

This chapter includes material from three previous articles: "From the Chaplain," *The American Organist* (June 2001): 10; "In the Image of God," *Journal of the Association of Anglican Musicians* (January 1996): 4–7; "Why on Earth Would a Church Musician Have a Spiritual Director?" *Journal of the Association of Anglican Musicians* (April 2001): 5–6.

1. Peter J. Gomes, *The Good Book: Reading the Bible with Mind and Heart* (New York: William Morrow, 1996), 214–15.

2. Evelyn Underhill, *Mysticism: A Study in the Nature and Development of Man's Spiritual Consciousness* (New York: New American Library, 1974; first published 1911), 301.

3. Ibid., 259.

4. Ibid., 239.

5. Athanasius, *The Life of Antony and the Letter to Marcellinus*, trans. and introduction Robert C. Gregg (New York: Paulist Press, 1980), 10–11, 16. I am grateful to the Reverend Dr. Richard Valantasis, professor of Ascetical Theology and Christian Practice at Candler School of Theology, Emory University, for his inspiring course on asceticism given during his all-too-brief tenure at Harvard Divinity School. See Vincent L. Wimbush and Richard Valantasis, eds., *Asceticism* (New York: Oxford University Press, 1995).

6. Samuel Rubenson, "Christian Asceticism and the Emergence of the Monastic Tradition," in Wimbush and Valantasis, eds., *Asceticism*, 49.

7. Richard Valantasis, "A Theory of the Social Function of Asceticism," in Wimbush and Valantasis, eds., *Asceticism*, 548.

8. Ibid., 550.

9. Howard Gardner, *Intelligence Reframed: Multiple Intelligences for the Twenty-First Century* (New York: Basic Books, 1999).

10. Ibid., 30–31.

11. Ibid., 41–43, 48–52.

12. Ibid., 53–66. Gardner is not ready to include existential intelligence, although he says, "At most, I am willing, Fellini-style, to joke about '8 ½ intelligences'" (66).

13. The exception was Professor Margaret Miles and her highly original work connecting the visual arts with historic Christianity. See Margaret R. Miles, *Image as Insight: Visual Understanding in Western Christianity and Secular Culture* (Boston: Beacon Press, 1985).

4. The Gift of Diversity

This chapter includes material from "Beyond Words and Music: Towards a Heavenly Discourse," a sermon preached at the American Guild of Organists New England Regional Convention on July 8, 1993, at First United Methodist Church, Burlington, Vermont, and published in *The American Organist* (May 1994): 80–81.

5. Silence

This chapter first appeared in "From the Chaplain," *The American Organist* (May 2002): 12.

6. Composers as Prophets

This chapter includes material previously published as "From the Chaplain," *The American Organist* (July 2000): 12.

1. Aaron Copland, *Music and Imagination*, Charles Eliot Norton Lectures 1951–1952 (Cambridge: Harvard University Press, 1952; fifth printing, 1970), 17.

2. Ibid.

3. Ibid., 18.

4. Ibid.

5. Ibid., 17.

6. Ibid.

7. The Book of Common Prayer, according to the use of the Episcopal Church (New York: Church Hymnal Corporation, 1986), 369: "In the fullness of time, put all things in subjection under your Christ, and bring us to that heavenly country where, with all your saints, we may enter the everlasting heritage of your sons and daughters."

8. Nicholas Hollander, Animaniacs cartoon *Piano Rag*, episode no. 30, originally released on September 21, 1993, Warner Brothers.

7. Ground Zero

This chapter first appeared as "From the Chaplain," *The American Organist* (February 2002): 10; and "From the Chaplain," *The American Organist* (December 2001): 18.

1. Bill Harris, *The World Trade Center: A Tribute* (London: Salamander Books, 2001), 8.

8. Worship Wars and Conflict

This chapter uses material that was first published as "From the Chaplain," *The American Organist* (August 2000): 10; "From the Chaplain," *The American Organist* (May 2001): 10; "From the Chaplain," *The American Organist* (November 2001): 34.

1. Donald Hustad, *True Worship: Reclaiming the Wonder and Majesty* (Carol Stream, Ill.: Hope Publishing, 1998).
2. *The American Organist* (August 2000): 10.
3. H. Wiley Hitchcock, *Music in the United States: A Historical Introduction,* 2nd ed. (Englewood Cliffs, N.J.: Prentice-Hall, 1974; first published 1969), 51.
4. Isabel Briggs Myers with Peter B. Myers, *Gifts Differing: Understanding Personality Type* (Palo Alto, Calif.: CPP Books, Consulting Psychologists Press, 1993; original edition, 1980).
5. Howard Gardner, *Intelligence Reframed: Multiple Intelligences for the 21st Century* (New York: Basic Books, 1999), 13, 41–42.
6. Ibid., 42.
7. Ibid., 42–43.
8. This passage is quoted as the source of the title for Myers, *Gifts Differing.*
9. Esther de Waal, *Living with Contradiction: Reflections on the Rule of St. Benedict* (San Francisco: HarperSanFrancisco, 1989), 30.
10. Ibid., 31.

11. The Association of Anglican Musicians, *Musicians Called to Serve: A Handbook for the Selection, Employment, and Ministry of Church Musicians,* 2004. AAM Communications Office: telephone 859-344-9308; e-mail: *AnglicanM@aol.com.*

12. American Guild of Organists, *Professional Concerns Handbook,* ed. David Vogels. The AGO also offers Boston and Seattle chapter work and compensation guidelines. Telephone 212-870-2310; e-mail: *info@agohq.org.*

13. Hans T. David and Arthur Mendel, eds., *The Bach Reader: A Life of Johann Sebastian Bach in Letters and Documents,* rev. ed. (New York: W. W. Norton, 1972), 125.

14. "From the Chaplain," *The American Organist* (May 2001): 10.

15. "There's a wideness in God's mercy," The Hymnal 1982, Hymn 469 (words: Frederick William Faber; music: *St. Helena,* Calvin Hampton).

9. Our Humanity

Sections of this chapter appeared as "In the Image of God," *Journal of the Association of Anglican Musicians* (January 1996), 4–7; "From the Chaplain," *The American Organist* (October 2000): 10.

1. Léonie Rosentiel, *Nadia Boulanger: A Life in Music* (New York: W. W. Norton, 1982), 292.

2. Ibid., 292–93.

3. Translation from *TANAKH: A New Translation of the Holy Scripture According to the Traditional Hebrew Text* (Philadelphia: Jewish Publication Society, 1985).

4. Peter Gomes, *The Good Book: Reading the Bible with Mind and Heart* (New York: William Morrow, 1996), 165.

5. Ibid.

10. Working Outside Your Faith Tradition

This chapter uses material that was previously published as "From the Chaplain," *The American Organist* (April 2002): 10.

1. Abraham Joshua Heschel, "No Religion Is an Island" (1965), *Moral Grandeur and Spiritual Audacity,* ed. Susannah Heschel (New York: Farrar, Straus, Giroux, 1996), 237.

2. Ibid., 238.

3. Ibid.

4. Ibid., 239–40.

5. Ibid., 235.

6. Heschel, "What Ecumenism Is," *Moral Grandeur and Spiritual Audacity,* 287.

7. "God is our fortress and our rock," *Worship III* (Chicago: GIA Publications, 1986), Hymn 575.

11. Predictable Seasonal Tension

Sections of this chapter were previously published as "From the Chaplain," *The American Organist* (May 2000): 22, and "From the Chaplain," *The American Organist* (December 2000): 18.

1. The Ninth Annual Worship Workshop, sponsored and hosted by St. Michael's Episcopal Church, Richmond, Virginia, November 7–9, 2003; co-sponsored by Union Theological Seminary and Presbyterian School of Education, Baptist Theological Seminary, and the American Guild of Organists.

12. Death and Dying

This chapter uses material that previously appeared in "From the Chaplain," *The American Organist* (April 2000): 20, and "From the Chaplain," *The American Organist* (July 2001): 10.

1. Thomas A. Dorsey, "Take My Hand, Precious Lord," *Lift Every Voice and Sing II: An African American Hymnal* (New York: Church Hymnal Corporation, 1993), Hymn 106.

2. Gwendolin Sims Warren, *Ev'ry Time I Feel the Spirit: 101 Best-Loved Psalms, Gospel Hymns, and Spiritual Songs of the African-American Church* (New York: Henry Holt, 1997), 178–79.

3. Ibid., 178.

4. Melanie Svoboda, SND, *Traits of a Healthy Spirituality* (Mystic, Conn.: Twenty-Third Publications, 1996), 13.

13. Should You Quit?

This chapter uses material previously published in "From the Chaplain," *The American Organist* (August 2000): 10.

1. Call the local chapter of the American Guild of Organists and ask how to get on the substitute list. If you do not have the number of your local chapter, call AGO National Headquarters at 212-870-2310 (e-mail: *info@agohq.org*).

14. Final Thoughts

This chapter includes material previously published in "From the Chaplain," *The American Organist* (September 2001): 10; "From the Chaplain," *The American Organist* (March 2002): 12; "From the Chaplain," *The American Organist* (May 2000): 22; and "From the Chaplain," *The American Organist* (July 2002): 35.

1. Paul Hume, "Keepers of the Gate," an address at the opening of the American Guild of Organists National Convention, Washington National Cathedral, June 28, 1982, published in *Cathedral Age*, the quarterly official magazine of Washington National Cathedral.

2. Nancy Roth, *The Breath of God: An Approach to Prayer* (Cambridge, Mass.: Cowley Publications, 1990), 20.